One Odd Cat

Strange Adventures in Strangeness

Larry Nocella

Also by Larry Nocella

FICTION

Four Weird Tales of Horror

Razor Wire Karma

The Katrina Contract

Loser's Memorial

Where Did This Come From?

It Never Goes Away (short and essay)

—

DEDICATION

Book dedications are a strange tradition. I don't like them. I don't do them. If you wrote the book for a specific individual, then why are you sharing it with others? But tradition requires it, so let me say this book is dedicated to whomever is reading it. As it always should be.

Thank you, dearest reader. I hope you will consider reading this book to be time well-spent.

Table of Contents

DEDICATION iii

1 A Note About My Wife, Heather...................................1

2 The Urinal Prank And Its Merciless Vengeance 2

3 The Skipped Birthday Incident.....................................5

4 Life Inside The Whack-A-Mole...................................10

5 Bespoke Bigotry: Bingo Bozos 13

6 My Standard Jokes For Standard Situations 18

7 Fear The Taker Of Notes...21

8 The Final Voyage Of The Starship Fantastic: How I
  Defeated A Depressing Workplace With A Tricycle
 26

9 Left Turn Improv Theater..32

10 What I Learned From Catching A Foul Ball With
  My Butt 35

11 BTSD: Below The Shoulder-Dancing – Stealth
  Mobile Raves 40

12 Moroccan Boss, Irish Grand-Boss, Language And
  Culture..43

13 My Brief Tap-Dancing Career 48

14 Sinbad The Sailor, Barbara Bush, and Life Lessons
 51

15 Air Guitar Contest 54

16 Jerks Might Be A Good Thing 57

17 Idea! An American Royal Family And/Or A
   Cheerleader Corps 60

18 When Rage is Funny: Couscous on the Loose Loose
  63

19 Survey Sabotage 66

20 Gandhi & the Drag Queens 70

21 Blaming Star Wars for My Foolishness 78

22 Pretzel Seduction 84

23 Let's Beat Up My Uncle! 88

24 Sports Radio versus Public Radio 91

25 Important Questions about the Climactic Ending of
   "Dirty Dancing" 95

26 One Last Blowout Above the Fold for Headline
   Artisans 98

27 Nostalgia Fail: Video Games 101

28 A Weekend of Protest and Motorcycles 104

29 Touching Each Other's Behinds Before Time Began
  111

30 Wearing a Dunce Cap on a Halloween Night City
   Stroll 113

31 Coffee, Chips, Karma 117

32 Boxing Champ Belt-Holder Guy Interviews for a
   New Job 119

33 Fighting Against Missionaries – Knives Only 122

34 Acronyms and Mnemonics 126

35 The Hidden Agenda of Stupid Trouble 130

36 Decoding The Extremely Difficult to Understand Difference Between "Reply" and "Reply All" 135

37 Notes for King Solomon on his Split-the-Baby Decision 138

38 Good Omens, Bad Dreams, Dog Poop 144

39 The Value of Lies in Church.................................... 148

40 All Hail Sasquatch, Zen Master of Cryptids 155

41 My Spokesperson, My Hero 158

42 The Later Years of the Kid Who Yelled at the Emperor.. 161

43 MOMS! And Kids! 163

44 I Don't Want to Civil War with You, Bro 167

45 Death and/or Homicide While Playing "The Penis Game" 173

46 Arlo: One Odd Cat.. 176

47 One Night in Sexyland... 197

48 Searching for Humor 215

49 Thanks All Around... 217

1

A NOTE ABOUT MY WIFE, HEATHER

Many of the true-life adventures described here involve my wife, Heather. She's awesome and I love her. She has a sense of humor more demented than most folks.

You will find in here a lot of jokes involving her, and her jokes about me. She has accepted this for at least 30 years as of this writing. There's no reason to stop now.

Other than her, all names are changed or obscured to protect the privacy of the people in the tales. She volunteered for this. Everyone else had better sense.

2

THE URINAL PRANK AND ITS MERCILESS VENGEANCE

Gather round, young ones! Let me tell you about a barbaric time when we worked in an office.

Can you believe we used to share facilities to manage bodily waste alongside other people? Complete strangers? Even homophobes and transphobes! Ew! Gross!

Back then, there was a type of person who would use the men's room that I'll call a "urinal talker."

Let me describe this strange creature.

Most bros just urinate at the urinal. If they're feeling chatty, they wait until they and others have finished and are handwashing to begin a conversation at the sinks. Some, however, talk while you are both "doing your business."

It's not evil, just annoying. Like posting on social media that you are leaving social media. Like cutting pizza with scissors. (For any doubters, yes, I've seen it done. I remember being at a party as a teen and horrified when the host's mother did that. I've never been the same.)

To feed my desire for light-hearted revenge on annoying urinal talkers, I would apply a simple prank-based action.

The moment would begin like any other urination.

I would be minding my own business. If luck failed me that day, a urinal talker would arrive, violating another unspoken rule by using the stall right next to me.

Normal and sane people understand implicitly that if there are more than two urinals you put at least one between you and everyone else present. Primal instinct instructs most people to urinate as far as possible from every other currently urinating person in the world.

Urinal talkers are immune to that logic.

The prank begins when I'm unlucky enough to have one of these folks stride up next to me. The newcomer stands in an adjacent urinal and begins pissing. I am doing the same.

Then, he starts small talk.

Side bar: At one workplace, there was a repeat offender. I fear this urinal talker was also hard of hearing because he would talk so loudly. He would arrive next to me and ask, "HOW YA DOIN?" at such a ferocious volume, his voice would echo against the tile surfaces of the restroom. It was startling, so much so I would execute a tiny leap, which — I probably don't need to say — is not a good thing to do when you have your work slacks opened and your junk out dispensing liquid waste.

Anyway, nice guy, but with an irritating habit.

Back to the prank.

The urinal talker would partake in some light

conversation, and I, captive and unwilling, would engage with him in some light small talk. You know, weather and sports. Then I would finish up and wash my hands quickly while still carrying on the discussion.

If all goes well, I'm now at the sinks, and the offender's back is to me as he continues to drain. We're still enjoying some light banter. Then I drop some open-ended bro question like, "What do you think Coach A should do to improve Sports Team B's chances of victory?"

While the target responds, I quietly exit. File under, "Irish exits – Special locations."

A good result is when the victim keeps talking, then turns around only to realize he was talking to himself alone in the restroom.

An even better result is if, as I leave the restroom, another person (or persons!) enters. Then the newcomer(s) arrived to witness some dude urinating while carrying on a conversation with himself like some above-average weirdo.

That's the urinal prank.

Agenda-driven, harmless fun at its best. And now, mostly obsolete.

As I write this, humanity has evolved to the point where one doesn't have to visit an office as much to earn a wage. So, my urinal pranking is largely over, as I'm in a public restroom much less often.

Oh, I miss those days!

Actually, I don't.

3

THE SKIPPED BIRTHDAY INCIDENT

It was Gene's birthday. Gene is not his real name, but it was still his birthday. We were all gathering for dinner to celebrate.

There was only one problem: I was playing Halo, a very popular game for the Xbox videogame system.

Back then, I was addicted. I would stay up all night playing it. Even on work nights, into the wee 1am-2am-3am hours. Then during lunch break, I would nap in my car to catch up on the sleep.

I can't remember if it was Halo 2 or 3. For those who don't know, it's a game where you play a future superhuman soldier shooting waves of aliens as you try to save humanity.

The game gave players a ranking based on wins and losses. I had forever been trying to get to level 50 and now, suddenly, with the worst timing imaginable, I had teamed up with other players online and as a group we were doing well, crushing opponents.

My rank kept climbing.

I was at level 49 thanks to joining up with this squad of elite space marines.

In the real world, my wife Heather was livid.

She kept screaming that we had to get ready, that Gene and his husband were going to arrive at any second. Then we would carpool with another couple for a fun dinner party of six to celebrate Gene's birthday.

But I was in the zone. I had a goal. I was going to see it through.

"If you don't go," Heather fumed, "Then you explain it to Gene! I'm not covering for you! I'm not saying a thing!"

Making everything more tense was the fact that Gene is one of those people who loves to be loved. He was one of those needy inhabitants of social media, where he demands others repeatedly confirm that he's absolutely fabulous.

If you didn't like one of his social media posts, you would hear about it. He would notice and complain in a frightening passive-aggressive way. His whining about such things sounded like good-natured ribbing but contained an ember of genuine rage.

Making this all worse was that Gene was a terrible photographer. He would often post a snap of his meal at an overly expensive restaurant, but he didn't use the flash right, didn't edit the photo with filters or coloring or anything to make it look appealing. The pictures were consistently mediocre at best, and the food, more often than not, would resemble the unnatural green-brown of cat vomit.

Gene would reliably add a glowing caption.

"Truly a wonderful lunch! Delicious!"

Don't you dare mention that it looked like barf-in-a-bowl. You had best like that post. Better yet, love it, and comment about how jealous you were and how yummy it looked. Failure to do so meant you were in BIG TROUBLE WITH GENE.

So, daring to skip his birthday dinner was an unprecedented danger with unknown but surely horrific consequences.

Meanwhile, in my video game, I was getting closer to level fifty, this arbitrary goal of mine that I had been obsessed with for weeks. Months, even! Maybe over a year! I can't remember.

Then Gene and his husband arrived.

By now, Heather was absolutely burning with fury.

Between games, I ran downstairs and hurriedly explained the situation to Gene. I am an honorable man (sort of) and I take responsibility for my actions, however dumb they may be.

I told him face-to-face.

"Hey, uh listen. You have to understand. I've been trying for a very long time to accomplish this goal in my video game. I finally found some people to team up with where I might be able to do it."

Now that I think about it, this is not the greatest reason to skip a friend's birthday party.

But I should get points for honesty, right?

I didn't really want to go anyway, game or not, so that made it easier.

Heather insists that as I was explaining it all, I was batting my eyelashes and using my self-described natural good looks and imaginary effortless charm to influence him. I can honestly say, if that happened, I didn't do it on purpose.

But if I did, that was smart!

We all suspected Gene had a harmless crush on me, and thought I was a cute guy. I needed all the help I could get to convince Mister You-Must-Adore-Me that

I would be skipping out on the celebration of him. For a video game.

Somehow, against all odds and reason, it worked. Gene reluctantly agreed to not get mad.

Maybe I caught him by surprise. (Likely.)

Maybe I'm just that good-looking. (Unlikely.)

Maybe it was my honesty. That I told him face-to-face. (Doubtful.)

We don't know why Gene didn't explode right then and there. Heather says that as they drove away without me, that she told Gene she was surprised he wasn't angrier. She was annoyed he wasn't furious and that once again, I had gotten away with my rogue behavior.

"I wasn't mad at first," Gene said. "But as I think about it, I'm getting madder."

That sounds ominous.

Well, um, Happy Birthday!

Anyway, this could be one reason we don't talk to Gene anymore.

Many years after the skipped birthday dinner incident, after apologies were made and accepted and the whole event was nearly forgotten, we were surprised to discover Gene and his husband had blocked us on all our social media accounts.

No warning. No explanation.

We never reached out for one. Gene and his husband never provided one.

We were tired of Gene and his self-centered ways. We haven't spoken since.

In retrospect, this was not my finest moment. It was a symptom of a growing addiction. I had become obsessed with a digital achievement inside a video game. At my age!

I felt bad for a long time.

But when we were suddenly blocked by Gene and he

had called off our friendship without any obvious or stated reason, I felt vindicated.

See? I was right to skip his birthday. He was a jerk all along.

It's true that two wrongs don't make a right.

But it's also true I got to level fifty.

4

LIFE INSIDE THE WHACK-A-MOLE

Doot-doot-doo-doot-doodle-doo!
The music! It's starting again.
I just wanna jump!
Me too! I'm getting an irresistible urge to leap up!
BONK!
Ouch. Someone is up there with a mallet!
I don't care. I just can't sit still!
BONK!
Ow!
Doot-doot-doo-doot-doodle-doo!
You ever wonder if there is anything more to life?
Wait. I gotta jump! Ha! Missed me!
What do you mean?
Like to existence. Is there anything more? Why are we here?
Don't be— Hold on, be right back!
BONK!
Ouch! Don't be ridiculous.

It never occurred to you to ask, why?
Doot-doot-doo-doot-doodle-doo!
Why—
BONK!
Oof! Why what?
Why do we sit here for hours on end? Why does the
music start and fill us with an uncontrollable
compulsion to leap in place? And why do we jump only
to get whacked in the head and knocked down again?
Or missed entirely? Why jump up at all?
I don't know.
Some good questions, though.
I never gave it much thought.
Wait a sec—
BONK!
Ouch. You're crazy.
He's been hit in the—
BONK!
Dang!—head too many times.
You never wondered? What's the point? Why not just
stay down?
BONK!
Ow! I don't know. It's just what we do.
My turn! Ha! Missed!
See? It's better to not be bonked in the head, right?
Keep asking those questions—
BONK!
Ugh!
Something bad will happen.
Why do you say that? What will happen? If it doesn't
matter, if there's no reason, why not stay seated?
Doot-doot-doo-doot-doodle-doo!
Now that's—
BONK!
Damn it! That's dangerous talk.

But why? Why would—
BONK!
Why would it be? That's it. I'm going to try It. I'm going to just sit here, see what happens.
Better not.
But there has to be a reason.
You sure? You're just going to sit there?
Aren't you getting the urge?
I am. But I'm resisting it.
What? You're crazy.
Doot-doot-doo-doot-doodle-doooooooo-wam-wammmm!
Hey, the music stopped.
Wait! Look at this!
Whoa! What's happening?
The sky is opening!
Bright light! Bright light!
See? I knew there was something else!
But what?
He's floating away, up into the air. He's gone!
Here comes a new mole.
Hello everyone.
Hey newbie.
What's up, rookie?
Welcome.
Where did the other guy go?
He stood up for something.
Actually, he stayed down for something.
You know what I mean.
Doot-doot-doo-doot-doodle-doo!

5

BESPOKE BIGOTRY: BINGO BOZOS

I'm a relaxed fellow. At least, I try to be. I'm very much against getting enraged about things that don't affect me. Fashion choices, hair color choices, who someone loves, which mythology you believe, and so much more are things other people spend time getting angry about that I find completely none of my business.

I try to embody "live and let live" as much as possible. Even for people I find repulsive.

I am always puzzled by people who work extra hard in finding abstract reasons to dislike others. Racists, homophobes, bigots, etc. never made sense to me. From a purely logical standpoint, why dislike someone if you don't have to?

Sadly, I do harbor one exception.

There is one thing that enrages me in other people. Even though it technically has no bearing on my well-being and doesn't harm anyone. I feel bad about it but console myself this way: I'm a human being. It would be unfair to expect anyone to be completely free of this common failing. Of course at least one breed of person is going to get on my nerves, no matter how hard I try to be universally chill.

Despite my best intentions, I can't help but find one group of people to be annoyed with. Enraged with, even.

Bingo Bozos.

Bingo Bozos?

Yes.

Bingo Bozos.

Adults who don't understand Bingo, the easiest game humanity has ever created. A Bingo Bozo is a person who calls Bingo while playing the game, even when they don't have it.

Strange, right? Why would I be so irritated when someone commits a harmless mistake?

I'm not sure. I'm only human, I guess.

My Bingo Bozo Bigotry was on naked display a few years ago when I attended my niece's grade school fundraiser Bingo night. There were a lot of children there in the eight to ten years old range, their parents were there, too. It was a rowdy night full of sugary refreshments and fun.

We bought Bingo cards and sat down to play.

And then, as usual…

AS USUAL…

AS FUCKING USUAL…!!!

Multiple times, adults called out Bingo, ran up to the stage and following a proof check on their card against the numbers and letters called, were declared to be, in fact, not winners.

Idiots.

Oh, stop it, you say. You're being too harsh. People make mistakes, they're distracted by all the kids running around. People don't pay attention, or they're drunk. They may have undiagnosed dyslexia. There's a bunch of reasons why someone might call Bingo when they don't have it.

It's not cool of you to hate them.

All true. All reasonable. Yet I still can't express sympathy for that type of error.

When the creator of your choice was handing out reasons to irrationally hate people, I must have requested the strangest one.

Let's see, we got the standard options that come free: skin-color, religion, place of birth.

Hmmm. Got anything weird? I'm looking for something exotic.

How about People Who Suck at Bingo?

My nice side tries, desperately, but still in vain, to put an end to my Bingo Bozo Bigotry. It tells my Bingo-Bozo-hating side to relax.

It never works.

My angry, unfair side responds: Bingo is not a difficult game. It is not a complex game. It is a slow-moving, basic, simple game. How can an adult screw it up and still be a functioning member of society?

RAWR!!!

My apologies for the outburst.

So back to the grade-school fundraiser. As usual, a woman nearby leapt up from the table and called out "Bingo!" She ran to the stage immediately to collect her prize.

Even the children all around us knew she was wrong. They chattered, expressing their concern.

I can still hear my niece's plaintive cry to my sister-in-law. "But Mommy! She doesn't have Bingo!"

The pain of injustice in her voice still breaks my heart.

You think that's unjust, kid? Wait until you learn about… well about everything else.

So this woman, this grown mature adult woman, who presumably votes and drives and raises children, walked up to the number caller and showed her card. And of course, we sat around doing nothing for several hours until the number caller finally delivered the verdict.

"Oh no, it's not Bingo, we'll keep going."

This happened multiple times. How? Multiple times! Yes! Every time!

Bingo Bozos!

At this point, the father of one of my niece's classmates and I began to share our disdain. Openly. Loudly. We then calmed it down because there's little benefit in being ejected from grade school Bingo. Not much rizz to harvest there as the kids might say, if the kids were grumpy middle-aged adults appalled at other adults who don't understand the rules of the simplest game of all time.

Once, during a fun virtual Bingo event at my day job, someone called out Bingo and was told they were wrong. TWICE. The SAME person. They should have been fired on the spot. If the event hadn't been virtual, I would be sitting in jail now for murder.

Let's end with a suspenseful tale.

My wife once shared a story of how as a child, she would score Bingo but not call it out because she was too shy. I find this tale a little sad and a lot adorable.

Years later, we were on a cruise and playing Bingo (made more fun with alcohol and marijuana gummies.) She scored Bingo and yelled it out.

I was pleased she had gotten over that childhood shyness, but that pride was soon submerged under a tidal wave of terror.

We had been married for decades.

What if she just called Bingo and she doesn't have it?

I stared in silent horror as the judges approached to check her card.

What if?

What if it is finally revealed that the keeper of my heart is a secret Bingo Bozo?

Was our marriage only moments away from ending?

What a strange way for love to die.

I could hear the drip-drip-drip of divorce lawyers back on shore salivating.

The Bingo officials came over. I held my breath as they checked her card. I stared into the abyss of an uncertain future and held my breath.

Eternity passed. They rendered the verdict. Her call was correct. She had won!

Better still, she had conquered her childhood fears. It was one of those times you gaze at your partner with pride and think, I made a good choice.

Especially since the prize was a few hundred in cash.

We immediately tore through it at the nearest bar.

6

MY STANDARD JOKES FOR STANDARD SITUATIONS

There are certain jokes and witty sayings I use and re-use in common, recurring situations. I call these my "standards."

I probably get this habit of re-using jokes from my father, who, while also charming, clever, and witty, tends to use the same gag line over and over. This habit caused me at one point to put a temporary ban on him using the old classic, "I'd use a cane if I were able."

Like him, I possess a collection of some stock jokes. Unlike him, I try not to use them to the point of annoyance.

Let's review these sure-fire chucklers.

1. When someone at the day job says, "you were right." I like to answer, "That's a first." This is funny because I'm usually right. And when I'm not I can provide an excuse as to how I was misunderstood. This joke is me

trying and failing to be humble. It's many layered as all good lines are.

2. When my wife and I arrive at a party and are greeted by the harried host(s), I will say, "Do you need any help? Heather's not doing anything." In this way, I am crassly offering my wife's labor to assist with the party chores whilst I enjoy and relax. This always earns a gentle laugh and a less gentle punch, as good-natured annoy-humor should.

3. This next one was a big hit back when the pointless rule of going to an office was in full effect. People would be gathering for an in-person meeting in a conference room, and I would loudly say something like "Oh, this must be to announce my promotion." Or "Oh, this must be about my raise." Most coworkers laughed it off knowing it was an obvious joke, but I took note of those who appeared jealous, annoyed, or shocked. The office jerks couldn't help but reveal themselves.

4. My personal favorite stock joke is when we relive the true story of how, during her high school teenage years and before she met me, my wife dated a boy who later came out as homosexual. I like to end the tale with, "I suspect she turned him gay. And some days, I feel like I'm hanging by a thread."

This last standard requires some backstory.

We once lived with a tiny Pomeranian dog named Wyatt. He was a show dog but whatever weird specs that show dogs must have, he wasn't having. His ears got too big or something, and his owner didn't want to "show" him anymore.

Silly, but whatever. A dog needed a home, so we adopted him.

He was a tiny five-pound dynamo, and just adorable. He was small but carried a huge personality. Those were his good traits.

His bad traits were numerous. He was very high maintenance. During night-time relaxation in front of the television, he would take up the whole couch, alone. Heather, myself, and our other dog Grace would crowd onto the loveseat. If anyone got near Wyatt on the couch, he would growl and run away.

Worst of all, Wyatt was very bitey.

He would bite for no reason. This led to tense times out in public where children would squeal with delight and want to pet the adorable little living toy. I'd warn them he would require a severed finger as payment.

Of course I'd say it a nicer way, like, "Oh he gets scared," or some other casual lie.

I expected one day we would be sued and forced to smuggle him into hiding to prevent him being euthanized for attacking a child.

We loved him, but we knew that he was awful and mean.

And so my standard line was the following.

"Yes, Wyatt was a terrible dog, he was nasty and barky and bitey, but it just goes to show, those of us who are good-looking can get away with anything."

7

FEAR THE TAKER OF NOTES

I once made the mistake of letting it slip at my corporate day job that I enjoy writing. I was promptly given the task of composing five versions of thirty-second radio ad scripts to sell used tires.

Fortunately, the task was not part of my regular work. I made up some excuses, pretended I was crazy busy in my main role and begged off the team.

I had escaped. It was a close call.

Lesson learned. Never tell them you have a talent. They'll put you to work.

But I'm not in the clear until I retire, because the same thing happened at another corporate job when it was somehow discovered that I can type reasonably fast because I enjoy writing.

I was assigned to take notes during the big weekly meeting.

Damn it.

My task was to summarize the topics discussed

during an hour-long conference call between multiple teams across different time zones, a few dozen people on each call.

This was before easy computer transcription, etc. Back in the days when there was someone who took "minutes."

At first, I dreaded this task. This was a genuine tragedy, and I was bummed about it for days. I would now have to pay attention to the meeting instead of daydreaming, doodling, sleeping with my eyes open, and/or thinking about stories I could write.

But as most things that I dread (and I dread everything) I soon realized it wasn't too bad. In fact, the keeper of the words has a quiet but formidable power. I was able to modify the record of what happened to my own benefit.

If you're saying, "Hey that sounds a lot like how the mainstream news media bends the news to always support corporate profits," you earn a gold star sticker.

The scribe has the power to alter collective memory, lead people's thoughts and write history.

When I wrote the meeting minutes, I was able to leave out tasks that were assigned to me. Even better, I was able to go into fine detail on subjects that would cause the jerks of the office to have more work. Best of all, when the jerks screwed up, I could highlight their mistakes with glaring clarity.

Oh, you want to me to take some notes?

Well then, imma take some damn notes!

People – being people and not naturally corporate drones – often quickly forget what was discussed or who was assigned what. That's all an opportunity for me, the note-taker, to control what happens next.

Being forced to pay attention, or rather, forced to appear to be, I learned some things.

I became attuned to folks who would talk a little and say a lot. There was one woman whose efficiency was impressive. I'm not being sarcastic (for once.) She would say her thoughts in a brief sentence or two. I would type her comments verbatim, and that would be it. I truly admired her skill and worked to emulate it.

I also begrudgingly admired the guy who was her exact opposite. This bro could talk for a solid ten minutes and provide five seconds of worthwhile information. Yet he never sounded like he was repeating himself. Annoying but still impressive! I would take down his one bit of info early on, but he would keep going and going, repeating himself in substance, but never using the same words. I ended up tapping the shift keys on my keyboard in furious rhythm to pretend I was trying to keep up with the verbal flood.

Of course, I did this to an extreme, tapping louder and louder, faster and faster. I got carried away with this gag to the point where my manager once reached over and rested her hand on my keyboard in a gesture of silent scolding.

She was cool, so I complied.

Lucky her.

But I would compensate with facial expressions. I would do things to pretend I was impressed, such as clutching my chin, or nodding with eyebrows raised, taking off my glasses and holding them to the side of my face. I would pose like a model taking stock photos around the subject of "Office worker, hearing a good point."

My co-workers got in on the fun. Since this was an audio-only conference call, we would play challenge games where we had to say a certain word like, "indeed" or at some point, hoot like an owl. We almost blew our cover by saying "indeed" far too many times than was necessary.

Indeed, it was getting weird.

Most of the time, I would be hitting the shift keys loudly and nodding my head as if I cared.

Eventually a "no laptop" rule was enforced. People were losing focus and playing on their computers. This was annoying because that's exactly what I would do.

When boring people got going and I was done my fake typing, I could surf the net.

With paper and pen, I could only doodle like a caveman.

One time, someone was babbling and as usual, I had jotted down their point in the first few seconds, but they kept droning on.

I sketched a face.

Then I added horns. Then I added sharp teeth.

My absent-minded sketch of a demon was coming along nicely.

I then added 666 in the creature's fangs.

"WHAT IS THAT?"

The guy next to me shrieked in the middle of the meeting, pointing at the sketch. I'm not exaggerating. This dude genuinely yelled out, startling me and everyone else. I was stunned silent.

Apparently, he had glanced at my notes and the horned creature with 666 engraved on his teeth. This sketch was so horrifying, so demonic, so offensive, that he had to yell and point at it. (For those who don't know, 666 is the number of the devil in the Christian Bible. Or not. Ask them about it. Some think it is.)

"WHAT IS THAT?" the guy next to me cried again.

Everyone looked at me.

"Uh, a scary demon?" I said, unsure. Then there was silence. Was he going to ask me to burn it or something? Was he some kind of religious freak and I was going to end up in Human Resources for attitude adjustment?

Everyone looked around for a while, but then nothing more happened.

I flipped the page to hide the horror from his prying eyes. The meeting continued as if there had never been an interruption.

After, I cut out the picture (it was smaller than your thumb) and showed it to my wife. She laughed and hung the picture in her cubicle.

See, we worked at the same place.

Which was a hell all its own.

8

THE FINAL VOYAGE OF THE STARSHIP FANTASTIC: HOW I DEFEATED A DEPRESSING WORKPLACE WITH A TRICYCLE

Now It Can Be Told: Why I Performed For Two Minutes On a Tricycle While Wearing My Beanie Copter In Front of Hundreds of Co-Workers and the CEO at My Old Job Many Years Ago

I was nervous, sweating, and close to passing out, but I had my mission, and I refused to fail.

I stepped to the front of the packed, humid ballroom. I was carrying a tricycle.

This was not a dream. The whole experience was utterly ridiculous, yes, but also horrifyingly real.

Days ago, I had purchased a cobalt-tipped drill bit and convinced a confused sales rep at the hardware store to help me drill through the trike's center shaft.

"This way it can support my adult body," I explained.

To my surprise and disappointment, he didn't ask any questions and immediately set to work helping me. Maybe he could sense larger forces at work, the approaching roar of destiny.

More likely he knew that talking would only keep me in his presence longer. Working together, I held the tricycle while he drilled the hole. We secured it with a nice hefty bolt so the handlebars could be raised and my knees could fit under.

That was days ago. But now?

Now was go-time, show-time.

I strolled into the cleared area of the ballroom that was the performing area. Right in front of the platform with the DJ setup and large boxy speakers. I set the tricycle down. The room was filled to capacity. Standing room only. Hundreds of my co-workers were there, and my boss. And my boss's boss, and so on several more times up the corporate food chain right up to and including the CEO. He was there, too.

This was the yearly corporate, mandatory fun event. I had volunteered for the talent show and had something special planned.

Wait. Scratch that.

I hoped something special would happen. Actually, I had no plan at all.

Talent performances were limited to two minutes. I just had to do something for two minutes. My hands were freezing but also sweating. My heart was thundering and my skin warm. Spots appeared on the edge of my vision. If I didn't get control of my nerves I was going to pass out.

I took a deep breath and put my foot on the tricycle.

I was, naturally, wearing my beanie copter. A symbol to indicate I'm in non-serious mode. Other than that, I was dressed in typical business-casual uniform for a summer company gathering: sneakers, khaki shorts, and a dark blue polo shirt.

Two minutes. I had to do something for two minutes.

Just do something. The problem was, I hadn't given much thought to what that something was.

The previous act (a woman who sang some karaoke song) ran from the performing area.

The D.J. introduced me.

"Now performing to Panama by Van Halen, let's welcome Larry!" boomed through the speakers.

Panama was the song I had selected.

All systems go.

Two minutes. How hard could it be?

Let me tell you something I learned that day. I'm not really sure this has application in anyone else's life, but you never know, so here goes:

When you are wearing a beanie copter and riding a tricycle accompanied by Van Halen's Panama in a ballroom filled with hundreds of your co-workers and the CEO of your company, and you have absolutely no plan for what you are going to do, two minutes turns out to be an excruciatingly long time.

So what happened?

I ran around like an idiot. I got the crowd clapping. Then I pushed off and rode the trike like a scooter. I leapt off the trike, did that Irish tap dance-thing, or maybe it was a Mexican hat-dance? I'm not sure. But whatever it was, I did it around the cycle and jumped back on.

And the rest?

Hell, I forget. More of the same, essentially.

Later, someone told me they were impressed with my song selection. Paraphrasing: "If you had selected a silly circus tune it would have just been goofy, but a rock song made it something special."

Another critic was less generous. "We all looked at each other and said, 'What the hell is he doing?'" she scoffed.

Word on the street was, that two of my managers jokingly argued over who I actually reported to.

Many moons later, someone asked me to name the performance, and I called it "The Final Voyage of the Starship Fantastic." Because it was a one-time-only show. It then became a point of importance to me that I give the tricycle to charity (which I did.)

Hopefully a kid somewhere is enjoying it right now.

I never rode it again, to ensure the fulfillment of the finality in the title of the performance piece.

Things like that matter to me.

I was mystified why I had been given the okay to perform at all. In previous years, people had sung karaoke songs with naughty words, so each act had to be first approved by a committee. I don't know why they approved when I smuggled my tricycle into the office to show them I was going to do something with it.

I was very vague about my plans, being as I didn't know myself, but they trusted me.

I wouldn't have.

But why did I do it at all? Was it a bet? How did things get to this point?

Why?

I get that a lot.

I often defer to a lyrical snippet from The Doors' song The Crystal Ship: 'Deliver me from reasons why.' Sometimes humanity's lust for reason gets in the way of enjoying life's craziness, of letting wonder and mystery carry you on its cosmic current, of riding along just letting things be.

On one level, the only answer is the rhetorical "Why not?" or the faux-mysterious "Because."

I'm not a fan of those answers, because I prefer a more precise approach. Also, neither non-answer comes close to the truth.

There was a reason for the silliness and an important one.

Let me explain. Yeah, about time! Some of you are yelling. Sorry. We're getting there.

First, an observation: have you ever noticed how people with an authoritarian bent are extremely annoyed by goofiness? By behavior they cannot understand or control? Especially if such behavior generates laughter?

The goal with my tricycle performance was to display a symbolic obscene gesture in the direction of those types. See, this workplace that was overrun by such beings. Not completely, as at the same time, I met many beautiful folks I am honored to still call friends these years later.

The place wasn't exclusively assholes, but it was infested with them, and they shared the traits I just mentioned: they were overly serious and full of superiority complex. Control-freakism ran rampant there.

As I've noted, few things enrage wannabe dictators more than someone who doesn't conform to their morose natures. It could be because laughter is something they don't enjoy, or because weirdness takes attention away from them.

Whatever the reason, random fun silliness infuriates them.

Yet random fun silliness happens to be my specialty.

What better way to mock these uptight jerks than to do so without them knowing? What better way to annoy them than by showing them that I was free and crazy and laughing and there was nothing they could do to change that?

Okay, maybe there's lots of better ways, but none so fun.

They would hate my tricycle "performance" for its unabashed absurdity, but in no way would they see it as a direct attack and invoke their petty wraths. Yet it would irritate them immensely because others would never stop talking about it. It would be so strange an event to occur in the context of a standard cube farm workplace that it would come up often, resulting in an itch the amateur dictators couldn't scratch, a bold expression they could not suppress with contempt.

So, did it work?

How the hell would I know? They were miserable before and miserable after.

As for me, I had a great time rising to the challenge and now I have this weird story. If nothing else, it was a lesson for myself. In the dark days of a miserable work environment, I thought I would never emerge. But I did and did so laughing.

My sense of humor — mystical, childish, and inexplicable as it is — saw me through.

Hopefully, you're feeling the silliness too and can share a laugh with me. Or at least you're a delightful mix of amused and confused. I'll settle for that.

I get that a lot.

9

LEFT TURN IMPROV THEATER

No one likes to be predictable. They like to be interesting and surprising. The most predictable thing in the world is that the instant you tell someone they are predictable, they will soon try to do something unpredictable.

Perhaps as an extension of this common desire, I am a huge fan of the silly non-sequitur.

Grapes.

I love things unexpected, harmless, and silly. Someone stumbling while walking behind a public speaker is funny, but a man in a chicken suit walking behind the speaker and then no one reacting, now that is super funny. At least it is to me.

Random events of the inane variety remind us that life can be a fun, magical, and ridiculous thing.

So many times we complain about the same old, we even have a bumper-sticker-ready and social media-friendly saying for it: same shit different day.

Based on all those observations, it's clear I'm not

alone in my contempt for routine. Random acts of absurdity are popular.

I'm leading off with all these observations as background for my explanation. I want you to understand why I make ridiculous faces while driving.

Pardon?

Let me explain.

For my non-existent readers in foreign lands, remember this story is told from the USA, where we drive on the right side of the road, and the driver is on the left side of the vehicle.

Imagine a four-way stop intersection. If I arrive from the south, and another driver rolls in from the west, and I make a left turn, I will pass very close to the other driver – my driver-side will roll right alongside his driver-side. We will be close enough to reach out and fist-bump, if we choose.

As my car comes around the front of theirs, I have often noted the dull expression on the waiting driver's face. They appear to sandwiched between grumpy and sleepy, like a kinky Snow White. They also appear a little bored.

Speaking of Snow White. There should have been a dwarf named "Bored." Then again, maybe there was but he stayed home. Obviously.

Anyhow, the stopped driver is clinging to the low-level annoyed impatient concentration that waiting at a stop requires. It's at this point, as I pass right next to the captive viewer, that my performance begins.

I will often make bizarre, funny, strange faces, scrunch my face, pretending I'm singing (or actually sing) make a shocked O face, and so on. It's all improvised with an emphasis on large expressions.

I offer this gift free of charge to my fellow human out of genuine good intent.

Random Acts of Kindness are cool, but I'm also a big believer in Simple Harmless Random Acts of Weirdness.

My goal isn't necessarily to make the other driver laugh, though I believe that will happen as they are reminded of how strange life can be. I want to snap the bonds of routine, remind them that the odd, the surprising, the disturbing, the fascinating, the inexplicable is always near.

They may be thinking consciously, "What the heck is wrong with that weirdo?" but unconsciously, their mind is alive with possibilities.

At least, I hope it is.

As always, when you try to make the world a better place, doubts creep in.

An internal voice scoffs at you: "You think that makes any difference?"

I once thought the same way. I've done this Left-Turn-Theater for some time and like most lost causes, I began to feel it was all for nothing.

Until!

Until someone I know, who I did not recognize at the time, was the recipient of my street theater.

When she confronted me later, she had many questions, all of which can be summarized as, "What the hell is wrong with you?"

She looked at me with confused amusement. I was partly embarrassed but partly pleased.

She was smiling as I explained.

She said she couldn't tell if I was singing or arguing or angry or what, but she was smiling.

I'm counting it as a win.

10

WHAT I LEARNED FROM CATCHING A FOUL BALL WITH MY BUTT

Being non-conformist should be done wisely. Many have observed before that if you just think the opposite of something on reflex, you're just as confined as a conformist.

You're "conforming to the non" as I like to put it.

Still, there are some clichés, some bits of common wisdom, that I resist because of their pessimism. For example, one cliché I don't like – but I must accept is true – is, "Life isn't fair."

I used to hate the idea of calling life unfair. It just seemed so… unfair. I tried to say that it was people that are unfair, not life, but that's wrong.

Some people are born with horrific diseases, that's not the fault of optional human action and poor moral choices. That's biology. That's life.

Fine. You win. I lose.

Life is unfair.

Now when it comes to calling life unfair, I burn with

the passion of the converted. I look back at my ultra-naïve, absurdly optimistic, youthful self and laugh with contempt: "You once believed in the Tooth Fairy. Even worse, you clung to the idea that life could be fair!"

What finally convinced me?

And what does this have to do with catching a baseball hit foul with my butt? Well…

Getting What You Don't Want
I've realized life is unfair by observing its consistent and annoying pattern of giving you things you don't want and keeping you away from things you do want.

For this story, let's review people's tendency to lose their minds trying to catch balls that go out of play (either by foul or home run) in major-league baseball games.

If you search the news, you'll find plenty of awful examples.

There's a story of a man who fell and died.

There's a guy who almost died, but other fans grabbed him and saved him.

There's a woman who stole a ball from a child.

There's a guy who dropped his child as he went for a foul.

There's plenty more examples of injuries and bad behavior as people chase baseballs. Do a search online and prepare to be horrified.

People really really really want to get their hands on a ball at baseball games. I don't understand it. Never have. It's a fun idea to get a free surprise souvenir, but not worth dying over, or acting like a horrible person for all to see.

It's just a ball.

I've always felt that way, and that's exactly why life, being the unfair jerk it is, delivered a foul ball to me with the greatest of ease.

Catching a Major League Baseball Foul Ball

Back in my early teens, my father scored some good tickets from his job. The seats were a couple dozen rows from third base for a Philadelphia Phillies game. It was a great day, just me and pop watching an afternoon weekday ballgame. I wasn't that into baseball. Never was, but it was fun just for the experience.

I was bummed the game wasn't televised. Being a kid, I wanted to be on TV!

The date was August 9, 1983. Philadelphia Phillies player Greg Gross knocked a pitch foul. Toward us. Everyone around us stood up. I felt confident it wasn't going to come near me, but I stood up anyway, to see what was going on.

The ball entered the crowd a few rows in front of me. Everyone was shoving and grabbing for it. The ball hit the back of someone's seat and took a crazy bounce. The feeding frenzy was on. People scrambled and flailed trying to snag the prize. In the chaos, the ball tumbled closer. After a bunch of weird bounces off people, chairs and the cement stairs of the stadium, just like that, the ball landed in my seat.

I sat down on it.

And that's how I caught a foul ball with my butt.

What luck! Totally awesome, right? Well yeah. It was fun and funny how it happened. Once the surrounding foul-ball-hunters sat down again, I grabbed the ball and stood up with it triumphantly. That's tradition!

It's also customary to show the lucky fan on the jumbo screen! Now that was something I wanted. If I couldn't be on TV, at least I could have that.

But whoever was running the camera for the jumbo screen didn't care to show me. People around went back to their seats, and the game went on.

Dang it.

But so what? You're saying. You caught a foul ball! Years later a man would fall to his death in front of his son trying to get one!

True, but I wanted to be on the jumbo screen! And I wasn't.

Life is unfair.

Being Lucky in Ways You Don't Want to Be and Unlucky in Ways You Want to Be Lucky

After the game, I gave the ball to my dad. He's the baseball fan. I've always been a follower of faster-moving sports, like... well, like anything. After years of my dad holding the foul ball he finally insisted I take it back. You caught it, he said, you should have it. And I still do. In a plastic box, in a cardboard box, under my bed, with a bunch of other junk, all safely encased under a fine layer of dust.

I can hear you now: you could sell it online.

I could. Online sales have created a reason for people to collect anything and everything, because surely someone else will pay more for it than you did, even if it is intrinsically worthless.

What's that? No, I didn't intend that as a critique of "investing" in gold, but yes, it does serve as one.

Anyway, yes, I could sell the foul ball. I could even donate the money to charity, but I won't now. It's become a symbol to me: a reminder that life is unfair.

It helps me remember that sometimes annoying clichés are true and that the grass is always greener on the other side. That the things you get so easily, someone else doesn't have despite all their desperate attempts to get it.

I think the trick is, for the things we want, we should

pretend we don't want them and sneak up on them. Then when life isn't looking, we make a quick grab.

But when isn't life looking?

It might just be easier to appreciate what we get, even if it's not what we want.

11

BTSD: BELOW THE SHOULDER-DANCING – STEALTH MOBILE RAVES

We were struck in traffic. Everyone in the cars around us looked bored.

We decided to have a dance party, but we didn't want to attract undue attention.

This rager would be exclusive to inhabitants of our vehicle only.

We would hold a dance party from the shoulders down.

From the neck up, our facial expressions would be the usual: staring forward, no expression, a little tired, a little irritated. Our lower body was blocked from visibility by the doors of the vehicle.

Unbeknownst to the drivers around us, we were pumping our fists and kicking our feet. It's a party from the shoulders down.

We've got a bad case of BTSD: below-the-shoulder-dancing.

What is the point of this?

The same as any party, to have a good time.

You're having a dance just an arm's reach away from another person who is stuck in traffic listening to used car ads on the radio, or yet another true crime podcast.

But why the exclusivity and secrecy? Why not just dance freely out in the open and maybe get people inspired with your infectious in-vehicle bacchanal?

Good question. I'm not sure. Let's throw out three possible reasons.

One, exclusive parties feel fancier. If only certain people are invited, you can see by contrast that other people weren't. The evil parts of human nature desire this inequality.

Two, we want to appear to the overseers of our capitalist wasteland that we are obedient worker drones. We want to seem slightly annoyed when we aren't earning them a profit. Secretly we are dancing away, having a good old time.

Three, I forgot the third reason. I'm too busy dancing.

I suppose for legal protection, I should say do not do BTSD: Below-the-Shoulder-Dancing while driving. Safety first.

Your passenger can keep the rave pumpin' while you are mobile.

But when you're stopped and you have a free moment, it's party time. Consider putting the vehicle in park, instead of your foot on the break. Your foot may come free during your slick BTSD moves.

You may think this is ridiculous, but you must admit the possibility that every single person around is doing BTSD and you're not. You simply don't know.

It's a sad metaphor for traffic, all so close, but no connection.

I prefer to pretend everyone is doing it. Everyone is

having fun, but they just look tired, bored, irritated.
Viva la revolution!

12

MOROCCAN BOSS, IRISH GRAND-BOSS, LANGUAGE AND CULTURE

I once worked at an office building for a corporation. What did I do? What do you think?

Excel, of course. Not meaning "be great at the job," though — ahem! — of course I did that. I mean, I used Microsoft Excel. I called my job title "Spreadsheet Jockey" which is what I call almost every job I've ever had. My survival has depended on my ability to move numbers around on a grid and then email that grid to other people.

I believe 90% of all office jobs (aka white-collar jobs) can be completed with a working knowledge of Excel. The remaining 10% are jobs you don't want.

Anyway, that's not the point. What I loved about this one Spreadsheet Jockey job were the cultures and folks it exposed me to. By luck of the draw, my immediate manager, my boss, was an interesting guy from Morocco. He had traveled to the USA on a student visa and decided to stay.

For the American psychos out there, yes, he "came here legally."

I had never met someone my age with a more interesting background. In defiance of the USA's unofficial past-times of hating Muslims and bombing their countries, I was eager to get to know him and make peace.

He was a wonderful guy, a good boss, and I learned a lot of Excel tricks from him.

He reported to another foreign-born individual from Ireland.

Hey American psychos, did you wonder if he "came here legally?" No? Well then, go think about yourself and don't come back.

Anyway, this Irish guy was also super nice and a cool bloke. When he heard I was being laid off from another department, my Spreadsheet Jockey skills proceeded me. I heard through the grapevine he was asking about my status.

This was a bummer for the part of me that always hates work, but fortunate for the part of me that has to pay bills. The Irish guy plucked me from among the cluster of folks being let go and hired me for his team.

Normally I would dislike someone performing such a rescue, but like I said, he was a good man. And I liked him. And I liked having money for food.

Working in the new team was a relaxed environment, but there was the issue of a language barrier.

See, the Irish guy was born in Ireland, and English was his first language.

I was born in the USA and English was my first language.

The guy born in Morocco, English was his third language (after Arabic and French.)

But the language barrier was not what you might

think.

The issue was I understood the Moroccan's English far better than the Irish guy's English.

The Moroccan guy had a faint accent that sounded lovely.

The Irish guy's accent was also lovely, but so thick, I could nary understand a wee word he spaekethed.

When I first heard him pronounce "Now" as "Nigh" that set off in my isolated American brain the bell of authenticity.

Wow, I thought, this guy isn't one of those creatures from the USA whose great-great-grandfather might have had an Irish sounding name and now they use that as an excuse to get wasted on Saint Patrick's Day. This dude says "nigh," when he means "now" — he's not American faux-Irish, he's real deal Irish.

The problem was, once he got going, I couldn't understand a word the guy said. If one of America's space-faring billionaires appeared before me and said, "I will give you ten million dollars right now if you can repeat word for word what that Irish guy just said." I would try with all my might … and fail, a fortune slipping through my fingers.

Irish grand-boss's accent was so thick, when he spoke to me and gave me direction, I found myself nodding a lot and then immediately going to Moroccan guy for a translation.

One might think having a boss one cannot understand is a good thing, but it was stressful because he was a nice guy. Or at least he seemed to be.

He could have been telling me to "fekuff" for all I know.

Fortunately, I reported directly to the Moroccan boss and he had significant cultural advantages over Irish Grand-boss.

For example, the best thing about him was that being Muslim, he would pray five times a day. He wasn't extreme (his words) but he did adhere to some common rituals of Islam.

Though he was great to work with, no one likes it when their boss is around. What if you knew your boss had to take a break a few times each workday to go pray?

That's an extra break for you!

Even better, during Ramadan, Muslims fast from dawn to sunset. Moroccan boss would be hungry and exhausted, not as sharp.

Let me say again, he was a wonderful human, but again, no matter how great your boss is, life is better when your boss is tired.

Yes, I do believe I might be going to hell for thinking these things.

Because Ramadan moves along the lunar calendar, sometimes the sunrise to sundown fasting occurred in the ultra-long days of the summer. This would be difficult and exhausting for him, as his fasting time would be extended.

Tough for him, but great for me!

Of course, this is the same place where I received a mild scolding for disrupting my cube farm neighbors. Apparently, I was laughing too hard from listening to prank calls on YouTube.

Hey, the work was getting done, though, right?

Yes, that happened. Me again, getting in stupid trouble.

I didn't want my earbuds privileges revoked, so I toned down my chuckling. It was a fair request and my co-workers were cool. I would have been annoyed too, probably, had one of my colleagues been enjoying the day so much, yukkin' it up while his devout boss adhered to his sacred tradition, and his grand-boss was off somewhere talking incomprehensibly.

I'll never forget those brief few years of work, where I learned more about foreign cultures than at any point in my life. It was a good time. As good as a Spreadsheet Jockey job can be.

Eventually, the continuing layoffs caught up with me. I was let go for a second time from the same company. I could take a hint.

There was no foul-mouthed incompressible Irishman, no soft-spoken Moroccan, to save me this time.

Oh well.

Sláinte and salaam alaykum.

13

MY BRIEF TAP-DANCING CAREER

My dust-covered tap-dancing trophy helps me recall the valuable lesson to never give up except when you want to quit.

Let me explain.

When I was eight, my friend began tap-dancing lessons. I suspect he was drafted because his sister was taking ballet and their mother found it easy to just send them both to dance class.

Somehow, I got drafted too. I can't remember why. Probably our parents had conspired to store all the kids in one place. How my younger brother escaped I'll never know.

I've never expressed an interest in dance as something to do with the intent of entertaining others. I like to dance like no one is watching, and it's probably best they don't.

Anyway, I didn't enjoy the tap-dancing and was relieved after our final recital.

I was glad to bow out. Mom seemed okay that I

wanted to quit. Exit stage whatever.

After our big show, they gave my friend a trophy, but not me.

I wanted one, too. I asked the teacher why my friend got a trophy and I did not.

You need perfect attendance, she said. You signed up after the first class.

I hadn't missed any classes, but because I joined one class late? Too bad. No trophy.

Damn it.

And so, I signed on for another season.

My final recital climaxed with a somersault. I rolled and jumped into a split-like touch-the-toes-mid-air move. Solo. No big deal. Huge applause. My neighbor friend's dad cheered my name.

"All right, Larry!"

Oh, stop, it wasn't that amazing.

Okay, fine.

Anyway, I got my trophy and promptly quit tap-dancing for life.

I still have that award, a six-inch tall golden figure of a tap dancer that can fit in my hand. I keep it as a reminder: persistence and discipline always win.

Never give up!

Right?

Not so fast.

In the years since, I've learned discipline requires a little soft-shoe. Persistence is good, having a goal is better, but knowing the exact measure of what you want is best of all.

I had a clear goal. I set that goal. I hit it, and then I stopped.

Clean and neat.

In a world of more and more and more and better and faster and more and expand and more, and how can we monetize this and how can we increase productivity and how can we go more and faster and more and nothing ever feels like enough, knowing exactly what you want is a valuable skill.

I wanted the trophy. I did what I had to do so I could get it.

And then I said, that's enough.

I don't think I've ever felt so complete.

14

SINBAD THE SAILOR, BARBARA BUSH, AND LIFE LESSONS

My wife once worked at a mall where Barbara Bush was touring for a photo op. Yes, that Barbara Bush, matriarch of the American political dynasty. Wife of one president, mother of another. As you can tell, we Americans have a long history of defying monarchies.

Anyway, a friend of my wife, a guy who worked at a bakery, made Mrs. Bush a cookie, just for her. As she strolled through the mall on a practice run, he offered it to her.

Allegedly (I'm probably supposed to add "allegedly" for legal reasons since this is just an anecdote) Mrs. Bush politely refused the cookie and said, "It looks delicious, but they won't let me have it."

There are different ways to interpret Mrs. Bush's words.

Maybe she genuinely didn't want the cookie and didn't want to hurt the man's feelings.

Or maybe, and I think more likely, because of her

high-profile position, she was wise to refuse food from a stranger. It might be poisoned. The "They" who wouldn't let her have it were her bodyguards and security team. Such is the life of the rich and powerful: full of distrust.

I like this anecdote for its muted sadness. It makes me think about cages made of gold.

We working-class folk look at celebrities and riches with such envy. They seem to have everything. But there is so much they don't have. They don't have trust, they don't have love. We don't see the price they pay for all that wealth.

I've said it before. Like nearly every word that emerges from my heavenly lips, it's worth repeating: Money has a cost.

When you're rich, gestures of genuine kindness are avoided for being too risky. Those around you can never be trusted, do they love you or do they love your wealth? People fake their entire lives, all in the name of being near power and wealth.

There is nothing some won't do for riches.

Absolutely nothing.

That's horrifying.

We working class simple folk know that the people who are with us are with us because they love us. Or at least, they aren't here for riches, because there ain't no riches to be had. The only real currency we have is love. Or at least trust.

And damn, we should appreciate that more.

The wealthy life that looks great from the outside doesn't seem so great on reflection. Less has a whole lot more to offer. The advantage of not being rich is that the people who are with you are more likely with you because of you and not your cash.

The real goal is to be rich, but appear poor. Then

you won't attract scumbag fakers of the highest order.

I first encountered a glimpse of this wisdom at the ending of the 1974 film The Golden Voyage of Sinbad. After Sinbad rescues the king and returns the crown to him instead of keeping it, his buxom princess friend is perplexed.

She asks him, "Sinbad, you gave away a whole kingdom, priceless treasure, why?"

Sinbad mansplains: "I value freedom. A king is not truly free. Why, he's even told who he must marry!"

I always liked that.

He could choose wealth or freedom. My man chose a free life. Cool, right?

Good call, Sinbad. Now marry that woman!

Sinbad the Sailor called it, back in the 70s, before Barbara Bush and the cookie incident.

The truth hasn't changed since then. If anything, it's only gotten truer.

There's pros and cons to every position.

You just need to appreciate where you are.

15

AIR GUITAR CONTEST

I always like to support local businesses and help others, so when our pals at the local tattoo studio were holding a fundraiser air guitar contest, I had to go.

Now before we begin this adventure, it's important you know about one of the tattoo guys whom we'll call Randy.

Randy is a crusty guy covered in tattoos. He has a kind heart but is one of those blokes who doesn't want anyone to know he's a nice guy. That's just his thing. He acts grumpy, but his social media posts of him caring for and supporting his daughter are adorable.

When it comes to Randy, because I like to get into stupid trouble, I like to "bust his balls."

Meaning, I like to do things to assist him in propping up his fake exterior. For example, I'll loudly ask him which teen bubblegum popstar is his favorite. Or request he and I go get mani-pedis as bros. Then he's able to insult me in some way.

I helpfully give him a platform to show off his

grumpy guy persona.

The tattoo-shop air-guitar fundraiser seemed a good place to continue this tradition. I figured the contest would involve people thrashing about as if they were being electrocuted mid-seizure. They would air-guitar to insane heavy metal tunes with blazing guitar solos that play 30 notes per second.

I decided that for a chuckle, and to annoy Randy, I would air guitar to an annoyingly slow, calm song. I chose the singer-songwriter classic "Longer" by Dan Fogelberg. This song has a super mellow guitar and lyrics that go something like, "Longer than... there's been whatever in the whatever... I've been in love with you."

I'm sure you've heard it... if you've ever been in a dentist waiting room in the 1970s like I was.

Anyway, the goal was to annoy Randy (who was one of the contest judges) and irritate the rough heavy metal tattoo crowd so badly that they would start throwing things at me and I would get booed and possibly assaulted.

It would be fun.

The bummer was this didn't happen.

Instead, I was up there on the stage of some bowling alley bar, strumming my air guitar like an aged hippie for the whole dumb stupid song. For its entire boring agonizing yawn-inducing length.

The judges, Randy, and the crowd were all respectful and polite.

Damn.

I didn't win the air guitar contest, but I got some swag for competing, like a sticker or something.

The next year, the air guitar contest landed on my birthday. That doesn't matter except to show how dedicated I was to supporting our friends and local businesses.

I could have spent the night being the center of attention, instead I helped the local tattoo parlor raise money while I was the center of attention.

To spice things up, I tried another singer-songwriter smash hit, hoping once again to irk Randy enough that he would react in some obnoxious way and cause a scene.

Again, nothing happened! Randy, the judges, the crowd... all respectful.

Damn it!

A professional irritant like me thrives on reaction and I was so irked that they weren't annoyed, I decided to elevate the performance. I ripped off my shirt midway through the song just to surprise, wow, and/or horrify the crowd.

All I got was mild applause. Maybe two or three "woos."

That was it.

These people were hard to agitate to the point of physical violence! What was wrong with them?

The next year... they did other fundraising efforts.

It was probably for the best.

I may have had to resort to punching one of the judges just to get them to throw things at me.

My air guitar career ended.

But there's always a chance for a reunion tour.

16

JERKS MIGHT BE A GOOD THING

I have a theory.

I have a lot of theories.

But I think this one is a winner because it brings me peace. Sort of.

I came up with it when I was trying to feel better about assholes. By "assholes" I mean jerks, not the actual physical anus, that exhaust port for expelling waste that every person has, whether they admit it or not.

Sidebar: Speaking of not admitting one possesses an anus, it's rumored that Kim Jong Un, dictator of North Korea, has such a stranglehold on the people that he demands they believe crazy things about him. One such myth is that he has no anus. I can't find any reputable news source for this rumor. It's entirely possible that he does push this belief, but it's also entirely possible that this is just "western" propaganda, intended to make foreigners appear extra weird and therefore more bombable than say, a dictator who confesses he does have an anus. It's very strange. Why bother with the propaganda? The war profit machine has such a lock on the US government, why do they waste time justifying a bombing? They could just do it, but no. Instead, they phone in the thinnest of excuses. Anyway, I refuse to do their bidding and spread unfounded rumors, so I'm not going to spend any (more) time on the idea that Kim Jong Un demands the people he oppresses believe that he doesn't have an anus. You have now fully read what is probably one of the more unusual sidebars in history.

Where were we before we started talking about Kim Jong Un's anus?

Oh yes. The presence of assholes and jerks. That is, people who act in ways you find repulsive, annoying, and cruel. Who purposefully avoid doing kind things and/or intentionally do mean things.

It's a bummer they exist, but I feel there's a reason for that. And it may be a good reason.

Because we have free will.

If you see a bunch of assholes around you, it is because when people are free, they will sometimes choose to be cruel. Therefore, while assholes around you can be annoying, their presence indicates that you live in a somewhat free society.

If someone is uninhibited to act in a way you find repulsive or annoying, then that person is not beholden to your belief system. You are not a dictator who can control their actions.

Even better: they are not the dictator of yours.

Rather than get mad at them, I choose to be glad they are free to be a jerk. Surely, I do things I find harmless fun that others find jerky. When I am just being myself, some others may think I'm being an asshole.

Because I'm not beholden to their beliefs, I am free

to act as I choose.

It's an adjustment of attitude. Next time someone cuts you off on the highway, or beats up someone at a sporting event, you can choose to get mad at them and lament the presence of assholes in our world.

Or you can choose your attitude and say, "Well, that's bad, but it's a good thing we are all free to act as we like."

Now, whenever I see someone acting like an asshole, I think, that's great! It's clear we live in a free country.

The only question remaining is: do we need to be THIS free?

17

IDEA! AN AMERICAN ROYAL FAMILY AND/OR A CHEERLEADER CORPS

Growing up American, I was taught by our culture to feel superior to the British.

They have a royal family. How silly!

Our national ancestors refused the tyranny of a social set where wealth, respect, and power were unearned and instead passed down by inheritance. We gave a double thumbs down to the idea that such people are considered worthy of our attention and adoration, regardless of their actions or character.

Describing this is hilarious because the USA, for all the bluster we were (and are) injected with, has a royal family. It's called the rich and famous. They're a social set defined by wealth, respect, and power unearned and instead passed down by inheritance. They're marketed as worthy of our attention and adoration, regardless of their actions or character.

You could argue that at least some of America's rich and famous are that way because they built a business, were somehow talented, or oppressed a minority so badly that they became rich and powerful enough to evade justice.

You could.

Making everything worse is the fact that in the USA, or perhaps, in every place there are humans, we have a surplus of people who want to be famous and not do a whole lot.

They crave attention. I'm not sure they even want to be loved. They just want to be known. There's no difference between famous and infamous for some of these creatures.

This sounds like a recipe for species that repeats the same problems every few generations. Those problems I refer to are how eventually it becomes obvious that these people – royals or rich – who by default are given respect, aren't worthy of respect at all.

But don't worry, I've figured it out.

Americans should establish a royal family.

Basically, we need a group of people who want the fame of elected office, or company executive, but none of the responsibility, empathy, talent, or intelligence that the best candidates for such positions possess.

A royal family fills the need for some people to worship — and be worshipped — but keeps them all away from the serious things like weapons, science, medicine, money, reason, logic, and decisions.

There are a whole lot of people who just want to cheer about the USA and say it's great and the best, no matter what the truth is.

Therefore, I propose a royal family of sorts for the USA. Being American, this can be decided by election. In keeping with current trends, it could be a televised voting contest with one minute of entertainment followed by twenty minutes of snarky judges offering their opinions.

The winning group will then, for a term of three years or whatever, be America's cheerleader team.

Now, I don't mean cheerleaders like in sports. I don't mean scantily clad, fit young ladies performing dance gymnastics. It would be quite the challenge to cram the average American into a skin-tight halter top and bikini bottom, let alone have them do a split. Can you imagine such outfits on the zombies of Congress? If you can, I recommend you don't.

What I mean is cheerleaders who only say positive things about the USA. The cheerleader squad will defuse the fascist instincts of many who embrace the "my country, right or wrong" attitude.

There are plenty of people being pointlessly famous now. They all demand they be taken seriously even though their only desire is fame.

I think the USA would benefit greatly from people who are paid to simply run around being the American Royal family, and saying the USA is the best, pursued by the paparazzi and featured in the tabloids.

Free up the spots in Congress for the well-meaning nerds who know book smarts and have good intent. Let the royal family cheerleading squad be for the people who only want the fame.

It's the only way to fix everything.

18

WHEN RAGE IS FUNNY: COUSCOUS ON THE LOOSE LOOSE

I often wonder about experiences that unite humans across space and time and culture.

Like what do we feel today that even Saladin's bootmaker or Genghis Khan's haberdasher felt?

Did they ever get so mad they kept on doing an action that they knew was foolish?

I think they probably did. That's human nature.

Have you ever had that feeling?

You're doing something, and it goes wrong, and it enrages you so much you just keep doing it.

Of course you have.

But back to me.

Whew! That was unbearable for a few sentences there — talking about others.

Anyway, I love couscous.

It's like pasta, but round, and small. A dot of chewy wheat. Delish! I used to love it so much I'd make it at least once a week. I'd make a nice big pot of it, mixed in my favorite vegetable (broccoli) and a pinch of salt.

So delicious and healthy! I couldn't wait to eat it.

So one time I had prepared a big bin of warm, salty dough pixels just waiting to be devoured.

I pulled the pot off the stove and...I dropped it.

Couscous went everywhere. All over the kitchen floor. I flipped out with the usual cursing and whatnot. My wife rushed in to see what the chaos was about, expressed her sympathies and offered to clean it up.

I responded like this:

"I'm sorry my dearest, but I refuse your generous and loving offer. Instead, I shall dine upon the couscous I have made directly from the floor, whereupon it lies."

That's not an exact quote. What I really said is rumored to have been more along this vibe: "You will not clean it up! I'm going to eat it off the fucking floor!" But you know, my memory isn't perfect.

My wife stormed off. I got a fork, knelt on the floor and scooped up the couscous into my mouth. It wasn't bad. Perhaps a bit too salty. Maybe that was from grains of dirt where we walked on the floor? The possibility crossed my mind, but I ignored it.

I was so furious about the spilled couscous, I ate it, dirt bits and all.

Knowing my wife was sitting in the living room nearby, stewing over the fact that I had yelled at her (though of course I wasn't mad at her) I made loud noises of ecstatic dining.

"Mmm! Yummy! Delish! Scrumptious!" I said, as I scooped forkfuls of floor-couscous into my mouth.

"You're an idiot," she said from the other room, assessing the situation correctly whilst laughing.

Good. If she saw the humor, as I was starting to, we could get through this disaster.

I apologized in the same vein as that famous line

from the movie Mommie Dearest, "I'm not mad at you, I'm mad at the dirt."

"I'm not mad at you, dear. I'm mad at the couscous."

I ended up finishing as much as I could, because I hate to waste food.

There are people all over the world starving, who would love a pile of couscous, on the floor or not.

19

SURVEY SABOTAGE

Back during the absurd era of my life called my college years, I took a psychology course. To complete the class, I was required to take part in experiments directed by graduate students. I made sure I picked the tasks that simply involved filling out questionnaires because I assumed those would be the easiest and fastest.

Unfortunately, the questions were long and deep. It would take a lot of time to read through the moral dilemmas and think about them. They would start with boring, detailed stories and scenarios, then you would have to make a difficult decision in a gray zone of morality.

For example, "You have a friend who needs to go to a funeral. But you promised another friend you would drive her to her wedding. Both are scheduled the same day. Which do you choose? How comfortable are you with this decision? Very comfortable? Somewhat comfortable? A little comfortable? Apathetic? A little unsure? Somewhat unsure? Very unsure?"

Being efficient, I skipped the stories and circled any old answer, making sure to select different ones. This created the illusion that I had read about and thought through the scenarios.

I completed the requirement in minutes, turned in my survey, got the credit, and took off for the nearest arcade. No one stopped me or asked how I was done so quickly.

It's for that reason that I've always been a little skeptical of polls, surveys, psychology experiments, and the like. Are the people taking them always sincere? Are they hurried or indifferent?

Or are they smart-asses like me?

Maybe I'm in the minority. Maybe, just maybe, most people aren't natural goofballs. When they agree to – or are obligated to – take a survey, they do so with the intent of being honest.

Me, I do so with the intent of getting it done and moving on with life as quickly as possible.

Plus, I never trusted psychology students. They're sneaky. They're always lying to test your reaction or setting up fake situations so you look like a jerk.

I'm not your lab rat, bro.

All that said, I love psychology. It's simply fascinating.

In my adult years, I still perform a variation of this survey sabotage.

It's weird for internet sites to include surveys now, when they can (and do) simply analyze my data.

But occasionally, I'll get a survey on a website that asks, "What brands are you familiar with?" Without hesitation, I click the None of the Above button because it's always at the bottom and the most quickly found.

I've wondered about this habit. Is it that the

cognitive commitment of ten seconds reading and thinking is just too much for me to bear? Or do I just naturally oppose doing chores? Or am I just a doofus?

None of the above? All of the above?

Then again, I'm often delighted when a survey ends with a freeform essay portion and asks, "Do you have any other thoughts?"

When I was immature, I would often fill in these online forms with short stories. I'd make some comment about my male anatomy and how it had just fallen off my body and I was in extreme pain in the moment and didn't have time to answer.

I've since grown up and stopped doing that.

Mostly.

Instead, I use the free-form section to add something like "Democrats suck but Republicans suck worse." Or some other quasi-public service announcement. If you're going to ask what I'm thinking, well, you might not like the response. That's not my problem.

Now my survey policy is much different. If there isn't a chance I will win a gift card or something, I skip it.

Of course, they could just be lying to me. Maybe there is no gift card prize for anyone. I risk it anyway using my speedy tactics mentioned above.

I take this approach to surveys at the day job as well.

I'm always puzzled when the corporate management bothers to ask if a pay or a bonus is adequate, or if the workplace is good enough. Am I satisfied?

No matter what you ask me, I'm going to answer in a way that I hope to manipulate your behavior. The goal, as ever, is to motivate the bosses toward paying me for zero work.

If I respond to "Was this year's bonus adequate?"

with "Yes, it was great!" then I feel that will communicate that they don't need to pay me any more money.

Even if I was offered a million dollars as a bonus and then surveyed about it, I would only ever answer that the bonus was "extremely inadequate."

20

GANDHI & THE DRAG QUEENS

No, it's not the name of a new band, or short-lived TV show, though it probably should be.

"Gandhi and the Drag Queens" was the theme of mine and Heather's five-year wedding anniversary. The adventure was a mix of deeply moving and goofy fun events. Just like our lives together.

I've always been fond of discord, of mixing things that don't normally go together. I'm a wannabe mad scientist. I keep hoping that someday I'll stumble across a winning combination.

Most things that make sense are being attempted, or at least advocated, and we're still flailing about in a sea of overlapping disasters. It's time to try a few random guesses.

Cape Cod, Massachusetts was our destination.

We had heard good things about it, we loved New England, and we wanted to visit a place called The Peace Abbey, a memorial to those who struggled for peace.

Plus, there was the lure of Provincetown, the famous gay-friendly party town.

The Peace Abbey

Warriors hog up most tellings of history because they aren't humble about their accomplishments. I suppose when you murder a whole mess of people, you want to explain yourself.

Peaceful folk are more, um... peaceful.

The Peace Abbey reflects this humility. It's a site with a monument and chapel, all dedicated to the cause and those who struggle for peace. It's so humble, it's easy to miss (though we went in the days before GPS.)

At the center of the Abbey's monument stands a statue of Gandhi, smiling. His hand is held low and is just begging for a high-five. Around him are several short brick walls, lined with profound statements from the usual collection of peaceniks.

There was no clear path through the abbey, and no map to explain what we could visit and see. As typical of peace movements, it felt a little chaotic. In contrast, the bad guys always seem so damn organized. I guess all that saluting and goose-stepping and forced conformity helps keep things orderly.

The positive side effect of chaotic layout is that it forces you to explore. We stepped into the chapel, unsure if we were entering someone's home. The walls were covered with inspirational quotes, stories and photos. A small chapel was made fragrant by incense.

Books on all kinds of ideas for peaceful change lined the pews.

It was a calming space. All these people, all these ideas from folks trying the best way to live kindly, to respect one another and our planet.

Yes. This was my team.

As we were leaving, I noticed that maybe twenty steps away from the peace monument, beyond a line of bushes, perhaps a very intentionally planted privacy shrubs, was a standard-issue war memorial to one of the USA's endless wars.

I wondered if the keepers of the Abbey were ever harassed about the proximity of their Peace Memorial. A suggestion for peace near a war memorial is a prime opportunity for rage enthusiasts to get angry.

Pop psychologists might call the placement of the Peace Abbey "passive- aggressive."

But where in this country could you put a Peace Monument that would NOT be close to a war memorial?

That says a lot, I'm afraid.

The silent Gandhi statue provides no verbal answers. He simply looks at you and smiles.

The only clue comes from the plaque beneath him which bears his immortal words, "My life is my message."

If you're curious, check out their website at www.peaceabbey.org.

...and the Drag Queens

Now that all that mushy meaningful stuff is out of the way, let's continue across Massachusetts to Provincetown.

Night in Provincetown on Saturday is a people-watchers' paradise. Commercial Street was packed. In full season, the crowds must be unbearable.

The vibe is accepting.

As person who truly believes in freedom, I am pleased when I know two men or two women, or anybody in love, can hold hands in public without fear of being harassed.

America, despite the intense marketing, is unfortunately not a place where gay couples are free from the random asshole, who would loudly complain (or worse) about them showing the most basic affection.

I felt a surprising burst of patriotism in Provincetown, thinking this is what America should be like. People should be free to walk the street and hold hands, and all the citizens, believing in freedom, realizing that who another loves doesn't affect anyone else, pay it no mind.

Every gay couple I saw holding hands filled me with pride at what a free nation could be.

On a lighter note, we were here to see a drag show.

Walking down Commercial Street, one is greeted with endless opportunities for dinner or some kind of theater. Finding a drag show wasn't the problem. Choosing one was the problem.

Today was the day on which, five years ago, we went to the local judge and swore that we would stay with each other forever. What to do on such a day? Walk on a beach? A nice dinner?

What would be a good way to celebrate our five year wedding anniversary?

Let's see a drag show.

Heather has always had a healthy respect for the films of John Waters. She's just plain odd and that's why I love her.

I was excited but nervous. I know drag performers often take great pleasure in making us hetero guys in the audience uncomfortable. Then again, I've always enjoyed this quote: "To do something when you are not scared is nothing. To not do something when you are scared is nothing. But to do something when you are scared — that is something."

When we got inside the theater, we kept looking at each other, laughing about the experience to come. Front row, drag show equals big participation.

The lights dimmed. In the darkness, I took a deep breath.

The show started with a queen dressed up as a jazz singer lip-syncing to a song and strolling down the center aisle, scanning the crowd.

When the lights finally went down, the man behind me whispered in my ear.

"She looked right at you! You're a dead man!"

I smiled in the darkness.

"We'll see about that," I thought to myself, accepting the challenge.

Gloria Estefan showed up next, and during her frenetic Latin dance moves, she pulled me up on stage.

I danced for all I was worth, which is not a lot.

I added a lot of hip-action on the assumption that such activity resulted in successful moves.

Then Dolly Parton showed up. It was a star-studded night!

She sang Whitney Houston's "I will always Love You" but switched the words to "Guys will always love my boobs," Then she came up to me, and spoke to me, mid-song.

The exchange went something like this...

"What's your name?"

"Larry."

"Do you like my boobs?"

"Very nice."

I'm not always a socially smooth fellow, but when a lady — or a man dressed like a lady — approaches you and asks "Do you like my boobs?" what else can you say?

Regardless, sometime during the discussion, she grabbed my head and smashed my face into her massive inflatable boobs. I flailed my arms about as if I was drowning.

I guess the crowd liked it... I don't know... frankly, I couldn't hear a thing.

I only know that when I came up for air, everyone was laughing and clapping.

"And now..." the announcer's voice said, awe-struck in the darkness,

"Marilyn."

The lights came up, and there she was. Marilyn.

In the meantime, every time a new celebrity took to the stage, a Loud Woman a few rows back would loudly say, "Oh. Beautiful. Perfect," as a way of was complimenting the queen's similarity to the celebrity in question.

I found it highly annoying. It turns out I wasn't the only one.

When Marilyn came out, the Loud Woman said it again.

"Oh. Beautiful. Perfect."

But this time, what sounded to like a very butch woman roared in the darkness.

"WILL YOU SHUT THE FUCK UP?!"

The whole place erupted into laughter and applause. So much so that Marilyn had to stop her show as she was upstaged by the thunderous clapping.

I felt bad for Loud Woman, but I agreed with Butch's sentiment.

Marilyn did too. "Yes," she said, waiting for the laughter to die down, "Yes."

I still feel bad for Loud Woman. She didn't mean any harm. She could have been quieter though.

Anyway, Marilyn asks whose birthday it is, a few

blokes raise their hands and are pulled up on stage to enjoy Ms. Monroe's wispy rendition of Happy Birthday.

As she and the two guys went past, she said, "And Larry, you come up here too."

Front row dammit.

Marilyn requested that the three of us each touch her breasts while we helped her sing Happy Birthday, which of course was terribly out of tune, ending with her banishing us from the stage with, "Oh, sit the fuck down. All of you."

The lights come up.

We're walking out and I hear, "Look. There's Larry, maybe we can get his autograph."

Magic in the Air

On our last night of vacation we were strolling the streets on our final evening in P-town. Suddenly Heather turned to me.

"Did you hear that?"

"Hear what?"

"Someone was calling your name. Larry. Larry."

I turned around.

"Let's go back."

But the voice was gone. We kept wandering, enjoying the hustle of a town getting geared up for a weekend we wouldn't see. Something was supposed to happen and we couldn't leave until it did. An eerie anticipation would not leave me.

It was supernatural.

Yet nothing happened. I felt incomplete, but since I didn't know what to look for, I finally said, "All right, let's go." It must have been my desire to be on vacation forever. That's all.

We walked back to our car along Commercial Street when a black SUV slowed down next to us. The window rolled down and woman in the passenger seat leaned her blonde head against the headrest.

"Hey, Larry," she said.

"Uh. Yeah?"

"You were great last night."

"I was? Oh. Well, thanks!"

"See ya later."

"Thanks. Bye!"

They drove away. Heather and I staggered on, bent over laughing at my micro-celebrity status. I raised my arms to the darkened sky.

"Thank you, P-Town!" I yelled.

Finally, I felt complete.

We left.

But a piece of my soul is still there.

21

BLAMING STAR WARS FOR MY FOOLISHNESS

Back before corporations were forced to admit that we didn't need to go into the office, I worked at a cube farm. Rows upon rows of gray cubicles filled a warehouse. The drab pathways reminded me of the trench around the Death Star from the original, the first, the best, 1977 Star Wars movie.

I would walk briskly down these pathways between the cubicles, and it felt like zooming down the trench in an X-wing starfighter. I imagined this as the showdown moment, when I needed to win or lose it all in an epic battle in space. It was a fun moment of imagination before getting back to my desk.

If you've seen any movies at all, then you know about showdowns.

They're moments when all or nothing is lost in a single instant. The good guy and the bad guy meet, and in a split second, everything is decided.

For years, I unconsciously believed a version of this

myth would play out in my life. I searched for the magic button to shut down my enemies (school and work.)

But I've learned since then that while there are pivotal moments, rarely, if ever, do you win or lose in an instant. Only in contrived situations like sports and videogames and fiction do showdowns exist.

In reality, you win or lose day by day.

Before I truly understood that I overlaid the showdown myth onto my life: if I could just write a best-selling novel, create some invention, program some app that would make me a millionaire, I'd never have to work again. I'd never be sad and anxious again.

I'd be happy forever.

I'm tempted to blame the movies for this foolish belief.

Obviously, I'd blame Star Wars, but I could also blame just about every single western ever.

It's not my fault for having a mental block, it's someone else's fault.

It was the culture around me that led me here. While I'm at it, why don't I give my affliction a name, like Showdown Anticipation Syndrome (SAS) and get big Pharma to market a pill that will cure it? The pill's commercials would portray happy people doing yoga in the park as a voiceover whispered the risk of appalling potential side-effects.

Seriously, there's no one to blame but myself. Nearly everyone has at least one obvious truth they have trouble getting around, one fact that blocks their path to Way Big Zen.

What I Learned from Star Wars

Star Wars said, half-symbolically, half-literally, that if you search your heart, put aside the technology and look within, you'll find some of the power that flows through all the universe (The Force) then you can do anything. This is played out as Luke destroys the death-star.

I love the part when Rebel Base senses Luke's switched off his computer and he's going to take the shot by feel. They ask him what's wrong and he says, "Nothing. I'm all right," trusting in himself. Chills. So awesome!

While I took hope from Star Wars, I also took too much.

Learning to trust yourself and search your heart, those were good things.

The idea that all your problems can be defeated with one amazing shot, absorbing the myth of the showdown, not good.

Yet I subconsciously learned that if you can just find the exhaust port, the central power source and blow it sky high, well then you're good to go. Nothing but peace and love, snacks and naps from then on.

How stupid that sounds when compared to reality.

But in Hollywood, it's everywhere: Locate the focus of power, make a powerful shot, and the Big Moment delivers a wowie-zowie explosion.

Psychoanalyzing this Hollywood trend indicates an unhealthy obsession with the male sexual climax.

Do It Yourself

So there I was in real life, hopelessly searching for the exhaust port, still waiting for that magic moment when the phone rings.

"Love your work, babe, want a million-dollar contract to do nothing?"

It took me a long time to realize there wasn't going to be a showdown, where I make the one-in-a-million shot and save the universe. There wasn't any golden ticket.

I left that bus stop and started walking.

As I moved through the years, away from Star Wars, there was no showdown. There was, however, a long study of inner peace. Imperceptibly it grew until I became the well-adjusted, always-content person I am today.

Sorry for spilling sarcasm all over the place.

The point is, I eventually learned that life has more in common with a confusing drunken mud-wrestling match than a quick and clean and definitive showdown.

That's probably a good thing, because you can adjust.

If life was like a showdown, and you lost, you'd be dead or have failed. Then you'd spend the rest of your life as a loser, unable to get good at anything else.

Innocence Lost

Equipped with this wiser attitude, along came a Star Wars sequel, the Phantom Menace.

It had been decades since the original.

I was so excited!

Then I saw Phantom Menace and was crushed.

Simply put, it sucked.

Like most Hollywood efforts lately, there was too much emphasis on visuals, not enough story. But what really let me down about The Phantom Menace was what it did to the myth of The Force.

My first concern (a bit superficial, I admit) is that the title sounds to me like the description of an exceptionally rancid fart.

Second, when are the bad guys in Star Wars going to learn not to use a centralized power source? Every single time, the good guys get at the "main reactor," destroy it, and the whole thing goes boom.

This reinforces The Showdown Myth.

Finally, and most annoying, when Anakin Skywalker (young Darth Vader) has his blood drawn, it turns out he has little particles in his blood called metaglobines or midi-chlorians or some other dumbass made up word. Those particles prove The Force is mighty within him.

What a catastrophic letdown!

In thirty seconds of movie time, the whole lore of The Force was destroyed!

No longer was it something one could master with discipline, no longer was it a power within each of us, that we could learn to wield with discipline and hard work, as Luke did on the Millennium Falcon in A New Hope.

The Force became a matter of heredity, like money. You were born with it, or you weren't.

In that moment, Star Wars ended for me. I've barely watched the many shows and spinoffs that have emerged since.

I chose to live forever in 1977, always a kid.

Still a Kid

I walked speedily between the gray cubicles at The Corporate cube farm. I was no longer just another cube jockey, but Luke Skywalker, blazing down the trench almost too fast - "Luke, at that speed will we be able to pull out in time?" - and I switch off all my computer gadgets - "You've switched off your targeting computer, what's wrong? Nothing. I'm all right." - and I search my heart - "Stretch out with your feelings" and I blast away.

"Great shot kid, that was one in a million!" cheers my guardian angel Han Solo.

And the whole damn Corporation, along with every other single problem I have, is blown to bits.

Figuratively, of course. Figuratively.

I have no wish to literally blow-up things and kill people, just escape oppressive systems.

I'm taken from my daydream, so I can make a quick turn before crashing into the water cooler.

Back to reality. Back to work.

The Corporation and our society built on overwork cannot be destroyed by one person with one amazing shot. It will take united action, and an altering of our entire culture.

Oppression exists not because of a lone person, but because he has a strong network. No single action is going to remove all those people from rebuilding what they want.

Keep struggling, of course, but don't expect a complete overturning, especially not an overturning with one swoop. That would be believing in showdowns.

And those truly only exist in myth.

May The Force be with you.

22

PRETZEL SEDUCTION

When I was in college, my friends and I lived in crappy apartments and had little money. A party was cheap booze, lousy snacks, and loud music. It was all we had but it was good enough.

Such was the time when I was courting my lady love.

On this lovely night we were, of course, at a party.

For entertainment, the hosts had loud dance music, cheap booze, and for refreshments, in the center of the living room (now dance floor) sat a huge box of pretzels. When I say box, I mean more like a tub.

It was big. Really big.

The hosts of this party, whoever they were, got this box at some warehouse or the university cafeteria — in bulk, cheap. The pretzels were likely on the edge of (or past) their legal expiration date and sold for maybe five bucks per twenty pounds.

The night continued and we got more drunk.

The girl I couldn't stop thinking about was there and I was doing anything I could to stay on her mind, to get her attention.

Our eyes met over the top of the pretzel tub.

Nothing was said verbally but a lot was being said of the flirty eyes variety.

At least from me.

I stood next to the bin, dipped my hand in and grabbed a pretzel, shoving it in my mouth. I'm not sure if this was intended to be sexy.

Anyway, still gazing at her lovingly, I grabbed another pretzel. Being drunk, my chomp was off target and sloppy. The pretzel splintered and pieces fell back into the box.

She laughed.

I had her attention! Perfect!

I grabbed another pretzel, bit into it, leaving some of it remaining. Then I purposefully tossed the remainder back in the box for community consumption.

She laughed harder. This was working great!

If any of you remember the movie 2001 with the famous scene as the chimp learns to use tools, his mind evolving before our eyes while classical music thundered in the background, that was more or less what was happening here.

I did it again. Bit on the pretzel. Ate some, and the rest? Back to the bin!

And again. Chomp!

Half in my mouth, half falling into the community pile.

More laughter. It was working!

She liked it!

And today, we're married.

Still.

At least, as of this writing. The pretzel magic could have worn off by now.

But our story doesn't end there.

Many years later, I shared this cute anecdote of silly, stupid, intoxicated young love with a bunch of folks, and everyone laughed at the crass foolishness of it all.

Except one guy.

He was truly pissed off.

His face crunched up when I mentioned throwing back the half-eaten pretzel on purpose.

He angrily asked, "Why would you do that?"

Maybe he was a germophobe. Or maybe he was the type of uptight person who cares about things like hygiene and sanitary food practices. Maybe he just didn't like love.

Whatever the reason, it tells me he is unfamiliar with life as a college kid. But the ickiness of it is what makes it funny. I was being obnoxious because it made a girl I liked laugh. Because it got her attention.

Still, this poor fellow did not see the humor.

He did not like it.

If this story offended you as well, let me say, yes, I realize it wasn't good behavior. Maybe it was even gross. But I won over my life partner with it, so you're all just going to have to deal.

If you don't like it, don't eat from giant vats of pretzels in the middle of a college campus party where there's no cups, spoons, or other tools and you must grab the snacks with your dirty hands.

Now that I write it all out, I would avoid such a thing now.

I like to think that my flirting tactics have evolved. But after marriage, maybe they've atrophied.

With horror creeping across my soul, I realize, maybe my flirting skills have gotten worse.

I wouldn't know.

I haven't flirted in decades. For anyone looking for a soulmate, consider that public vat an invitation. Before there were dating apps, it worked for me.

23

LET'S BEAT UP MY UNCLE!

I don't know exactly why but I never really had the instinct or desire to have children.

Now, as required by law, I am obligated to follow that up with a reassurance that I am not some kind of monster who doesn't adore your spawn, no matter how fucking annoying said child(ren) is(are).

And as also required, I am to agree that yes, your kids are unique miracles.

Just like all the other millions of unique miracles.

Seriously, I get it, parents. I truly do.

Being there for the birth of my niece and being her favorite uncle (her words) has been one of the greatest joys of my life.

It's all the administrative stuff that my sister-in-law had to do that I wanted to avoid. I went to high school. I don't want to guide another human being through that nightmare. Once was enough. I don't want to buy clothes for a kid. I did that when I was a kid. Well, my mom did but you know what I mean. I want to try new things in life, not repeat events I was glad to escape.

Being the crazy, fun uncle was and remains a joy.

My sister-in-law takes this dreary child-rearing stuff all very seriously and did (and continues to do) an outstanding job caring for my niece. She crushed it when it comes to the raising stuff.

That's why I don't mind doing my part for the fun party stuff.

I'm all about sacrificing for the wee ones.

Like the time my niece's seventh or eighth birthday was held at a movie theater. We were in a room with a cake. And that was it.

All the adults and all the kids were crammed into a colorful room with gifts and a cake and not much else. Nothing to do before the movie started. The theater didn't do much to entertain the kids or provide anything fun for them while waiting. I realize now this may have been the sister-in-law's fault, but I am smart enough not to mention that out loud.

For fear of not just her wrath, but her sister's. You try telling them they screwed up something.

Anyway, the children were bored. It was time for super uncle to do something.

But what?

While I was thinking, my niece decided it would be a good idea to start punching me.

The other children jumped in.

Only a lifetime of training in good manners prevented the adults from joining in. I have that effect on people.

Anyway, within seconds, I became the party favor. These tiny piranha children began attacking me, hitting me, pulling at my clothes, climbing on me.

The other adults sat by and laughed.

I sacrificed myself for the joy of their violent kids.

As the beatdown continued, only one of our friends expressed concern for how rough the children were being.

Only one.

But I shrugged off that concern. I reminded her I'm a badass street fighter, a wanderer of the wasteland, a space marine. I'd seen far worse than this during my hours of playing video games.

These little ones couldn't hurt me.

EXCEPT.

One girl was wearing these clog-like shoes with solid wooden soles. She enjoyed kicking me in the shin.

That hurt.

And she kept doing it. The other kids were hitting me, pulling at me, punching me, etc. I shrugged it off.

Except the girl with the clogs to the shin.

Clonk! Ouch! Over and over. Same shin, same place.

I didn't say a word in the name of fun.

I endured that pain all for the children.

See, I'm not so bad.

She's college-aged now as I write this. I hope she had fun.

Because If I ever meet her again, I'm going to kick her in the shin and ask how she likes it.

24

SPORTS RADIO VERSUS PUBLIC RADIO

For a long time, there's been an effort by the pro-ignorance factions of American politics to drain federal funding from public broadcasting.

Those attacks are obviously just one more tentacle of an authoritarian culture's desire to promote stupidity. The dumber people are, the less they will want to challenge, or know how to challenge, the powerful.

Public broadcasting's high-mindedness makes it an easy joke target for us cool kids, but that's why it deserves respect.

Yes, they're nerdy. Yes, they talk in that soft voice in an attempt sound smart, only to end up sounding like they're trying to not be heard, which is a weird strategy for radio. And yes, they focus on boring details.

But those details are important to make sure everything doesn't collapse.

When I used to drive around a lot, before employers were forced to admit office visits were completely useless (thank you, COVID19!) I was a captive audience for car radio.

After I had exhausted rock radio, I would often choose sports talk radio or public radio.

Both had pros and cons.

If I wanted to learn about the world, I would tune in to public radio.

If I wanted to learn how the world truly operates, I'd listen to sports talk radio.

Let me explain the difference.

On public radio, a topic is discussed. People call in and sincerely express their viewpoint, which they have given a lot of thought to. Everyone is civil, and passion is shunned to a fault. Raising your voice is enough to disqualify your argument. Everyone listens to everyone else and assesses ideas thoughtfully. Logic is respected. Facts are revered. Education, intelligence and experience are given credit.

But public radio is the only place in life where that sort of thing happens.

On public radio, people listen, they reason about the topic and assess truth.

It's the way things should be.

But for a lesson in the way things are, I listen to sports talk.

What's respected on sports talk – especially Philadelphia sports talk – is attitude, volume, passion, and the ability to entertain. In the end though, those things mean nothing in the face of power, which is held entirely by the host or producer. That is, the mysterious unknown person who decides who gets on air, and whoever controls the microphone kill switch. It's not unusual for a caller to be cut off if they manage to say something that embarrasses the host.

On sports talk radio, "You're an idiot," is enough justification for dismissal of an opposing view. "You suck," is adequate articulation. Passion is stoked and baited. Shows will often have their hosts take unnaturally opposing views just so callers will jump into the argument.

After just a few listens, it's obvious much (or all) of the controversies on sports talk are simply theater designed around one goal: keeping listeners' attention and selling that attention to advertisers. This was engagement bait before social media.

Sports talk is a more accurate model for how most people act, and how civilization works.

Oddly enough, the range of opinions on sports talk are far more diverse than public radio, again providing a more accurate model for humanity.

On public radio, each caller's values are roughly the same. They want the best solution to a situation that is logically an agreed-upon problem.

On sports talk, people hold opinions based on values that are wildly different. They may hate (or love) a team because of the colors of their uniform, or because that team loses (or wins), or because someone on a rival team is a jerk (or a nice guy). They may dislike (or like) someone because they have a moustache, or an annoying (or beloved) significant other.

Arguments go on despite there being no point to the arguing. No one's beliefs are based on anything other than opinion, so the arguments are endless.

As a naïve young lad, I once thought along the lines of the public radio model.

I thought that having the right facts would be sufficient to convince people of anything those facts indicated. Showing them the pain and/or damage their actions caused would immediately convince them to change their ways.

It took my naive, optimistic mind a while to adjust to

the reality. Most people are rarely, if ever, motivated by facts. They're not motivated by empathy. They are in their own world and they only change when they decide to. They don't even change when all the facts, even facts they're aware of, indicate they should.

All our shiny gadgets and grand achievements and the lizard-brain still has enormous control.

Some people respect power and only that. Facts mean nothing. For these folks, their only currency is fear. They are any authoritarian movement's members and victims at the same time.

Listening to sports talk radio was (and remains) for me a free education in the lizard-brain lifestyle, handy for practice in understanding irrationality, the ecstatic thought-free freedom and horrifying stupidities that go with setting difficult logic aside. In other words, humanity.

It is no surprise that public radio is under constant attack.

Public radio values being correct over volume, and that annoys the crap out of power seekers (and power submissives).

To the lizard-brain, gravity, climate change, whether the sky is blue, these aren't facts, these are all opinions. Everything is opinion.

Public radio is one of the very few places that provides the valuable service of not exploiting our lizard-brains for profit.

I've learned a lot from it, but to truly understand the world, I listen to sports talk.

25

IMPORTANT QUESTIONS ABOUT THE CLIMACTIC ENDING OF "DIRTY DANCING"

Dirty Dancing is a famous movie.

Like many famous movies, it's very cheesy. Overwrought. There's lots of emotion and not much logic to its simple love story. Bad boy gets girl, bad boy loses girl, bad boy hoists girl over his head.

But I have some questions.

At the end of Dirty Dancing, the character played by actor Patrick Swayze invades a gathering of rich people. He charges the stage, and interrupts the meeting. He then gives a vague speech about things he's learned despite a hard life. He wins the crowd over, then super-wins them over with a "Dirty Dance" and the ritualized pagan offering of the maiden to the sky god or some shit.

Even the grumpy dad villain does a complete reversal, from hating the tough guy to accepting that he's boning his daughter.

Who knew all he had to do was lift her up in public?

Like a caveman of myth, dragging the girl away by her hair.

Take note, bachelors!

The entire sequence was puzzling to me.

First, Patrick, that was rude, stepping to the microphone.

Second, why is no one shoving him aside? Grabbing the microphone back? Where the hell is security? They were having this rich-person party, discussing whatever rich people talk about, such as how to distract the poor with culture war bullshit and keep their minds off income inequality. There was some light entertainment, then this rough-n-tumble workin' class dancin' hunk jumps up on the stage and steals the show quite literally.

Then the most unbelievable thing happens: Rich people become sympathetic.

They choose to care.

They make no move to re-establish order or have their guards crack skulls. Nope. They all, collectively, silently agreed. They just accept it.

Then again, Kanye did this to Taylor Swift in the infamous "Imma let you finish but Beyonce had the better album" music award thingy incident. She never lunged at him to grab the microphone back, and no security tackled him.

Which makes it smell like a pre-arranged stunt, but who knows?

Maybe it's something primal among us primates. Whoever has the talking stick has the power. Eventually people learn that if you simply grab the talking stick with force, you can silence others.

How did THAT become a solid metaphor for how government and the media work?

Anyway, Swayze pulls a Kanye and everyone just

accepts it.

"Oh, I guess this is what we're doing now," the assembled rich folk seem to say. "We were discussing financial returns and enjoying some light entertainment, but that's over. Now we're having biography time with the hired dancer."

It's always bothered me.

Why didn't they call the cops?

"Hello, emergency? Hey, there's this dancing guy who took over our meeting. Get over here and beat his ass. We're rich, so move it!"

Nope.

None of that happens. They earn respect for him. They listen to what he says. They sympathize.

It's weird. And I am sad to say, obviously, absurdly fictional.

I can only conclude that doing something similar in real life is okay. And based on the Kanye-Taylor Swift-Beyonce thing, this conclusion is backed up. Rushing the stage and grabbing the microphone so you can complain about your life is completely safe and acceptable.

I'm going to do it somewhere soon.

26

ONE LAST BLOWOUT ABOVE THE FOLD FOR HEADLINE ARTISANS

By the time you read this, I don't know if there will be any newspapers left.

Headline writing, "above the fold" will be a lost art.

Even worse, all headlines written for websites will be composed to comply with algorithms and search-engine optimization (SEO).

If you are reading this is in the time before every headline to every story regardless of the article's subject is something like "The One Great Thing about Boobs and Puppies and Crypto That You Can't Afford to Miss" then you will understand the jokes here.

You see, my child, back in ancient times, there was nothing more a paper-based headline writer enjoyed than titling a story with a clever pun, wordplay, rhyme, or obscure reference to some cultural item.

Headline writing as a profession, and its clever sensibility, will be a skill lost to time, just like the ability to exist and not be enraged every second.

As a tearful gift to this soon-to-be arcane artistic expression, I reversed the sequence for maximum joy.

That is, I made up news events that would be a headline-writer's dream.

NEWS EVENT: A woman quits her job as an executive at a banking firm to sell candies from a shack by the ocean.
HEADLINE: From the C-Suite to the Sea Sweets.

NEWS EVENT: Three of all beers in a six-pack test positive for diarrhea-causing bacteria.
HEADLINE: Sick of One Half a Dozen of the Other

NEWS EVENT: Parents clone their terminally ill child. The child miraculously recovers, but the parents spoil the clone and ignore the original.
HEADLINE: Everything Happens for a re-Son

NEWS EVENT: Would-be thieves are thwarted by an amateur gardener and his aggressive pet parrot.
HEADLINE: A Bird in the Hand Beats Two in the Bush

NEWS EVENT: Deranged destitute French man, Charles Leon, arrested for masturbating in park
HEADLINE: Now Po Leon Bones Apart

NEWS EVENT: Large container ship becomes unmoored, crashes into dock, as Captain blames everyone else for the incident.
HEADLINE: Captain Cantankerous

NEWS EVENT: Pimp arrested for assaulting a John who vomited on a sex worker.
HEADLINE: Duck My Sick

NEWS EVENT: Sexy Men's Underwear Model Alfonso Rivera rumored to have injected buttocks with fish bacteria to preserve skin flexibility and youthful appearance.
HEADLINE: Super Fish Al

27

NOSTALGIA FAIL: VIDEO GAMES

When I saw the original movie TRON in the early 1980s, the main character Flynn (played by Jeff Bridges) lived in an apartment above an arcade.

I thought that was the coolest thing ever. At any moment he could go downstairs and play video games as much as he wanted.

Now those primitive games of the 1980s can be crammed by the thousands onto a simple thumb drive and purchased for a few bucks. It's a childhood dream come true.

My immature nature does well to hide my actual age. You may not guess, but yes, I was around for the birth of arcades in the early 1970s and their golden age in the 1980s.

The Atari 2600 home game console changed my life. I was mesmerized by the idea that you could live out adventures on a screen. I even learned computer coding at a young age and sold my first computer program at fourteen (no big deal.)

LARRY NOCELLA

Games then, especially home games, were extremely basic. You were a dot, or a series of dots to form a blocky tank, spaceship, race car, etc. It was a simpler time. But it was all we had and we loved it.

Now, games are lifelike. A quick glance at the screen of a current video game and you might mistake it for a real video with real humans.

Back to now. When I first learned I could purchase over 100 old Atari 2600 games for less than a single modern game, I was amazed. Could this be? Outside of owning an arcade and living in the apartment above it as Flynn from TRON did, my younger self never even thought that was possible.

I never even dared to imagine it.

Of course I bought that compilation in a split-second. My heart soared!

Every single game I had ever played as a child was at my fingertips. On demand! As an adult I could take a whole week off work and play as much and whatever I wanted!

Wow!

I fired up a game.

The screen flickered. The blocky tank moved across the blocky landscape made with two colors.

Blip-beep. Bloop.

This was it! I was playing one of the old-timey games! No parents to tell me to stop, no school to attend. My time was my own. Amazing.

But then something happened.

I couldn't help it.

A thought entered my mind thirty seconds later, unbidden, reflexive, and horrifying.

These games suck.

I was not entertained. I was bored.

The games were awful compared to today's life-like

action. They lacked the ability to play against other people on other continents. They lacked battling AI enemies that were eerily smart. They lacked realistic sound and soundtracks so moving that you could listen to them as stand-alone albums. They lacked actors voicing the characters providing deep, thought-provoking stories better than many movie plots.

I powered down the compilation.

Games have improved.

Significantly.

It turns out I'm not a nostalgia kind of person.

It was a dream come true.

But those were dreams for my younger self. The things I wish for today are much different.

Now I'd like an entire week not to play videogames of my choosing but to sleep all day every day without that nagging feeling I should be doing something.

Can that fit on a single USB drive?

28

A WEEKEND OF PROTEST AND MOTORCYCLES

Scheduling Conflicts

Life is annoying.

Weeks and days pass where nothing exciting happens.

Then suddenly, you have opportunities for fun activities and they both occur the same day.

This happened to us in the year 2000. Almost, but close enough.

The two events missed each other by a day. We would be able to attend both, given enough sugar and coffee to keep us going.

The first event was scheduled when a bubbly work friend invited us to her husband's motorcycle club's yearly party. Out in the Philadelphia suburbs we had heard whispered legends of the riotous celebrations of Pennsylvania's rural motorcycle clubs. We were eager to attend.

The same weekend, the Republican convention was

taking place in Philadelphia. A protest was planned. We wanted to go there and remind them that they should care about the people. I'll leave it to you to decide if our efforts worked.

It was going to be an action-packed weekend.

The Motorcycle Club Party
It started with a trip out into the wilds of Pennsylvania.

We still have a plastic mug souvenir. For a small fee, you could get the mug and as much beer as you could drink. The cup read, "Riding into the Millennium" as this was 2000.

A friend later pointed out that Millennium was spelled wrong. There was only one letter L.

Millennium is a weird word. Why so many double letters? Why double letters ever?

I don't know, LARRY.

The rules of the festival required attendees riding their bikes (meaning motorcycles) onto the grounds.

No bike? You can still attend, but you must park your car off-site and take a bus to the grounds.

The shuttle dropped us off in a field and departed. The other folks on the bus disappeared into the crowd. We were left standing alone, wandering in circles, with no idea where to go.

Our friend who had invited us, while a sweet person, was a bit flighty and light on the planning. Then again, we didn't really pressure her for one. We never developed a solid idea how for connect, and since this was before widespread cell phones, we meandered around the bus drop-off area.

In the high school playground that is adult society, bikers and hippies have not always been compatible. My wife and I are definitely hippie-adjacent and I felt like we were sticking out and drawing negative attention for being so obviously confused. We were carrying collapsable chairs slung over our shoulders, looking like we had gotten lost – very lost – on the way to a folk music festival.

No one said anything, no one did anything against us. But in this unfamiliar landscape, I became more and more paranoid. Casual glances from other folks seemed infused with accusations and or distrust.

While looking for our friend, we heard the famous cry that many had told us about.

"Show me your tits!"

Men would call out at passing females. Some women obliged.

We even witnessed a new twist on that classic as a trio of ladies approached a man so wasted he could barely stand.

"Show us your dick!" they yelled.

He did, valiantly keeping himself upright, pulling his pants forward as camera flashes illuminated the gap between his drawers and crotch. He then staggered away.

Thank you for respecting equality, good sir.

Somehow, we found our friend.

In the dusk, on giant fairgrounds, with no planning, this was impressive.

And a relief.

Once settled in at the campsite, I started to relax. We had found our ambassador.

It was great to see people partying (drinking, smoking, riding motorcycles, eating, laughing, etc.) all in a celebration of freedom.

But there were some signs around the grounds that looked like they came from the nineteenth century, or from the skankiest corners of the internet. Some attendees, not all, but some, had decorated their pavilions with racist cartoons and even worse, swastikas.

This is the bummer of it all. These folks who value freedom above anything else, too often come attached with those anti-freedom ethics.

There is a wonderful live-and-let-live vibe to the whole scene, unless you're the wrong color.

* * *

We attended the famous "Beauty Pageant," which was essentially a wet t-shirt contest. The two finalists got to the end by forming an alliance and making out. Judging by the roar of the crowd, it was a winning strategy.

After wandering around, we sat in a circle around the fire, drinking booze and shooting the breeze. From where I was sitting, I was facing the dirt road that ran between the different campsites. And while we're chatting about any old thing, a completely naked guy rides by on his motorcycle.

Yes, completely naked.

Owing to all the campers and pavilions in the way, I was the only one who saw this.

I didn't say a word to our small group. I simply smiled in my head and my whole body was warmed by a peaceful feeling. I felt as if I had seen a beautiful lake in a valley surrounded by snow-capped mountains and no one else in the whole wide world had seen it. It was a gift from the universe for me and me alone. The chatter around the fire continued and I savored this hilariously strange vision.

I would tell the others about it later. For now, it was all mine.

A short time after — a shockingly short time — the

same guy came riding back the other way, still absent clothes. But there was one addition. This time, he wasn't alone. While he was riding the cycle, a naked woman was straddling him and facing the opposite direction.

Best rear-view mirror ever!

Yes, to answer your question. They appeared to be having sex while he was driving at least 250ccs of motorized vehicle. They rode into the dark distance and out of my view.

Again, I kept quiet and savored this scene, letting its uniqueness roll around in my brain for a while. Among my small group, again only I had seen this wonder.

It was time to share.

"You all won't believe what I just saw."

I told them.

There was a rushed shifting of seats for a better view of the path should more interesting events occur. But they never did. I alone experienced the odd joy of seeing something you don't see every day and will likely never see again.

I was overwhelmed with gratitude. Most people go their whole lives never seeing people having sex on a motorcycle in real life.

The conversation died down after a time.

Our adorably naïve friend, unnerved by the silence, chirped brightly, pointing at me and my wife.

"Hey, they're going to protest the Republican convention this weekend!"

Immediately, I was on guard.

Back then was a simpler time. At least it seemed so. We vegetarian hippies leaned Democratic and gun-loving folks leaned Republican.

With our long hair, in the dark, we could pass as biker people, but our silly friend essentially "outed" us as liberals who were not as pro-gun as those surrounding us. Normally this would just be a little awkward, but I was on edge and anxious in the context of the dark campsite and strange environment.

The joy of the sex-on-a-bike vision faded.

I held my breath. Was it wise to mix politics with beer, drugs, and bikers?

To my delight, it all led to a nice discussion.

They weren't as extreme as I had stereotyped them. They had the same approach as most Americans: guns are okay for hunting and self-defense, but they drew a line at soldier's weapons in civilian hands.

These days, Pennsylvania is a valuable "swing state" in presidential elections. It's a large population that cannot be relied upon to vote Democratic or Republican. It's up for grabs. In a way, I like that. Pennsylvania is a diverse place. And in that diversity, there's lots of cool things to see and do and people to meet.

There's a lot of reminders that other people have different views than you, but you have a lot in common, too. I just wish they would drop the racism.

The Next Day at the Protest

I wasn't entirely sure what we were protesting.

I had been to protests before – as I think every American should be at least once. I had protested fur, the circus, and other forms of animal cruelty.

This time the goal was just a matter of showing up and trying to remind the people in power they were supposed to represent our interests, not just their own, not just the wealthy.

I wanted to do something unique with my protest, maybe bring a little humor along.

Philadelphia had recently passed a law that people

were not allowed to wear masks at protests or rallies. I didn't know all the details. I think it was because during a serious vandalism crime, the perps were wearing ski masks. They were caught on camera, but because their faces were hidden, they couldn't be identified. The no-masks rule was put in place to provide a reason to arrest people ahead of suspected crimes.

Or something like that.

I chose to protest the anti-mask law in a non-violent way to honor greats like Dr. King and Gandhi. And I chose to do so in a humorous, smart-ass way to honor myself.

I made one of those old-school opera masks on a stick and held it in front of my face as my way of defying the new ordinance.

"I'm breaking the law!" I said from behind the bulging cardboard eyes, "Because I'm wearing a mask!"

Most people at the protest got the joke, and I received a bunch of laughs and compliments.

I even got on TV!

I was thrilled! It was funny to see myself on the evening news performing my mask-protest routine.

But if I think about it more, there were tons of serious issues people were trying to call attention to. As usual the news ignores all that and decides to air the best theater: a sarcastic clown with a cardboard opera mask.

The news isn't dog bites man, it's man bites dog.

That's why you shouldn't watch the news too much.

You'll think there are hordes of dog-biting men everywhere.

29

TOUCHING EACH OTHER'S BEHINDS BEFORE TIME BEGAN

Supposedly, a zillion years ago, all matter was once all condensed into a single point.

This was called the singularity.

There wasn't two of anything, there was only one of everything.

Before the big bang, every molecule that makes up me and you and everyone and everything was smashed into an infinitely dense point.

Crowded like you can't imagine.

Who knows how long it stayed that way, in that time of infinity, probably a mind-blowing amount of time. Then it exploded and expanded, and blah blah blah, skipping some details… here we are.

It's incredible to think of it.

Amazing.

Also disturbing.

Because it means that at one point our future lips were touching someone else's future backside.

No matter who you are, whomever you dislike most in the world, there was a time when your future lip molecules were touching the future buttock molecules that are now attached to the person you hate most.

I suppose the counterpoint to that horror would be this delight: your future hand molecules were also caressing the future face molecules of whatever celebrity you find the sexiest.

That's hot.

But it doesn't make me feel much better about being so intimate with the hated person.

I think what we've learned here is that many things are true, all at the same time.

Whether you're grossed out or excited depends on where you direct your attention.

30

WEARING A DUNCE CAP ON A HALLOWEEN NIGHT CITY STROLL

A friend was throwing a Halloween party.
She demanded we wear costumes.
She insisted. I resisted.
I'm not a person who enjoys fashion. Or dressing up of any kind, especially for Halloween. I like my clothes comfortable and ready for action. A guy like me must be ready to do a chore, fight a bully, or you know, sit on my ass without warning.

Worse than that, I've always had this fear that something important is going to happen on Halloween. Then I'm going to have to give a speech while dressed up in some embarrassing costume.

Say I dressed up for Halloween as a robot, wearing a cardboard box wrapped in tinfoil, with ROBOT across the front with a backwards R for extra fun. Suddenly, due to details that phobias don't bother to fill in, I need to get in front of a crowd of people and give a very sincere and serious speech. I'm nervous and I need to get it right. It's important. But there's no time to change into a suit and I'm in this ridiculous half-assed robot gravitas-draining costume.

I don't know how these circumstances might come to pass, how I might suddenly be called upon on Halloween to give a presentation with no time to change.

Random bouts of anxiety don't give a crap about probabilities. Or possibilities.

So that's the background.

That should explain why, when a friend invited me to her Halloween party, I kept saying that I wasn't going to wear a costume.

She threatened that if I showed up without one, I would not be admitted.

Now that I say it out loud, she had a point. It was a Halloween party, after all.

Anyway, I said, okay fine. I'll wear something simple. I made a dunce cap with a large piece of construction paper. It was an absurdly tall pointy hat with the word DUNCE written on it.

That was it.

If I needed to give a speech, I could easily de-costume and I'd be good to go in standard street clothes.

My companions were my wife Heather and a friend. I don't know if Heather had some half-assed costume. I can't remember. Our friend was wearing some weird makeup which I was afraid to mention. I wasn't sure if that was her costume or was just her makeup.

Our Halloween outfits, if they existed, were minimal.

We arrived at the sketchy basement apartment in the poorly lit streets of western Philadelphia. Being generous, there were maybe four people there. The host was sitting on stool near the door, bouncer for the event, as the other attendees looked up from the collapsed couch.

The host saw me and my mini-entourage and immediately began shaking her head no.

She also appeared to be drunk.

No, she said and shook her head again.

No.

As in, no, you are not permitted to attend my party.

I explained that we were wearing costumes, as promised.

I had my dunce cap. Heather had something I can't recall. Our friend had weird makeup.

Apparently, none of this was sufficient.

No, no, no, the host repeated. She had warned me. No costume, no entrance.

It crossed my mind to note that the party wasn't exactly a banger, what with so few attendees. I could have pointed out she didn't really have the luxury of turning away anyone who wanted to attend. But it was like arguing with a drunk person.

No. No. No.

At this point, the friend we came with, the one with the makeup that may or may not have been a costume, started arguing with the hostess. It quickly escalated to shouting.

Each was a friend of mine, but they were strangers to each other, suddenly in a loud argument.

I was appalled that they could so easily raise their voices at someone they had just met.

I'm not a shouter. When an argument reaches a certain high volume, I bow out. It's obvious nothing is going to be achieved.

I realize though, that some can scream at each other for days. These two were those types. We could be here all night. I backed away and the three of us left.

I was frazzled and annoyed. I needed to take a walk.

Heather and our friend retreated to a local pizza joint. I decided to go for a stroll to work off my irritation. In my disgusted and irritated attitude, I kept on my costume, the tall pointy dunce cap.

It was my fuck you to the world. A strange fuck you, but the best I could offer on short notice.

It didn't cross my mind that a lone white boy wearing a homemade dunce cap whilst walking along the dark streets of West Philadelphia was not the most street-smart thing I'd ever done. I was too annoyed, but looking back, it seems the dunce cap was a bit more accurate than I had intended.

And so I strolled aimlessly, burning off the frustration of being denied entry to a party, and the shouting, something that others did so casually but always jolted my nerves.

The streets were unlit, quiet, and lonely.

But my beloved sistas of Philadelphia did not disappoint.

As I walked by a couple, the two laughed.

"What's that shit on his head?" one asked the other as I passed by.

I kept walking.

She could have just asked me.

Eventually, I returned to the pizza place, met up with Heather and our friend, and we left the city.

It wasn't the best of Halloweens.

31

COFFEE, CHIPS, KARMA

I have always laughed at old people who complain about the array of options in a coffee shop.

"I just want a coffee," they grumble. "Just a simple coffee. I don't want a mocha-frappa-whatever latte soy whatchamacallit."

They get irritated at all the options and fancy words, a tactic made popular by Starbucks, mimicked by coffee shops everywhere.

There's no more small, medium, large. There's tall, grande, venti. Oh, that's exciting and new!

There's no just coffee, there's macchiato, espresso, whatever-o. It all sounds fancy (but it's not.)

European words (made up or real) drive Ugly Americans crazy. That fact is regularly exploited by cable news culture warriors supplying anger fuel to the dinosaur-aged demographic.

Meanwhile, the barista waits for the order.

"Do you want it with almond milk or soy milk? Would you like it blended or whipped?"

"I just want a damn coffee!"

Silly old people and their rage.

I laugh at them.

Ha! The world isn't so simple anymore, gramps! We have different flavors of coffee now. Look at all this selection. Isn't it better? Your primal ways are no more! You stuffy old stiff. Get with the times. Quit whining! It's our world now.

Having expressed my contempt, I have done my duty as a freedom-loving American.

* * *

Then one day I wanted chips. What the British call crisps.

Potato chips, you know? Slices of potato, fried, salted. Simple and delicious.

I just wanted some chips, so I popped into the store and found the chips aisle easily.

But there were no "just chips." They had sour cream, cheddar, sea salt and vinegar, barbecue, jalapeño.

But no "just chips."

I just want potato chips! No bizarre flavors. I don't want the spectrum of colors in my packaging.

They didn't have "just chips." They didn't have regular potato chips.

Sorry, gramps, the world isn't simple anymore. Choose a flavor. All this choice, isn't it great?

Curse you, universe!

How dare you come back around and make me feel the frustration I once mocked in others!

It turns out karma comes in many flavors.

32

BOXING CHAMP BELT-HOLDER GUY
INTERVIEWS FOR A NEW JOB

HIRING MANAGER: So, I see here you're applying to be a member of our Boxing Champ's entourage as the championship belt-holder guy. Impressive resume. At your most current employment, you carried the belt and held it up behind Megastar after his successful title defense.

APPLICANT: Yes, that was a tough one. He thanked God in English and Spanish for at least twenty minutes. My arms were shaking, but the job's the job.

HM: What would you say was your proudest achievement in your entourage career?

APP: Besides holding the belt, I also wore a baseball cap with his sponsor's name on it. Brim sideways.

HM: Really? While holding up the belt? At the same

time?

APP: Yes. There's video on my phone. It was to promote a testosterone supplement. He had an endorsement deal. Let me show you. (Pulls out smartphone, shows video.)

HM: Impressive work. That hat's brim is definitely not aligned with your face.

APP: Thank you.

HM: What was your most difficult task on the job?

APP: Megastar was getting bad publicity for not paying child support. After a match, I called ahead to alert the club to have 12 seats ready. Then I called the tabloids. When we arrived, it looked like they spontaneously rolled out the red carpet for us. Really, we just had reservations.

HM: What does that have to do with child support?

APP: Nothing. But it pushed aside that story in favor of the pictures of flashy people in a club.

HM: I see. Nice job! So why do you want to come work for us?

APP: Well, Megastar was also sponsoring a Crypto coin and I invested. All my money is locked up in that and you can't pay your rent with imaginary money.

HM: Ah, don't I know it. Tell me, what's your biggest weakness?

APP: I sometimes steal the drugs I buy for him.

HM: Aw hell, that doesn't count! You're hired.

(They shake hands)

HM: Ouch. That's a firm grip you got there.

33

FIGHTING AGAINST MISSIONARIES – KNIVES ONLY

I don't think a lot of folks who are into this religion thing realize how terrifying their myths are.

In the Christian Bible, God is a stone-cold psycho killer. He's wiping out entire cities, entire civilizations. All for a little too much partying.

He's sending people to eternal torture like he's popping jellybeans, one after the other, not a care in the world. And he's sending them to be tormented FOREVER. However long your life was, one slip and you get not just a little torture, not just torture for two or three times the average human lifespan. Nope. Forever. Eternal. An infinite multiple of your living life.

Seems a bit extreme.

But it's not enough for God. He's drowning us humans, turning us to salt, setting us on fire.

It's horrifying.

People make mistakes, but there can be no mistakes with the Lord. If you're in the same city being good as can be and God has a grudge against your hometown?

You're toast. Burnt, salty toast.

So anyway, during my religious training for the Catholic church as a teen, a nun shared a story.

In this tale, a priest was blessing the host. That is, he was formally declaring that the coin-sized bread wafer in his hand symbolized the body of Christ. As he was performing this important ritual, he was having doubts about his faith.

But God showed him a thing or two! He sensed the priest's doubts and transformed the wafer into a quivering piece of flesh.

Now, the teller of this anecdote, being a nun, was moved by this story as an example of the power and truth of God.

Now, me, being a rebellious teen, was terrified by this story as an example of God being a psycho.

I was so repulsed by this, that it set me on the path to doubting all Catholicism, climaxing with my nearly pure atheism as I write this.

But back to the tale of the faith-impaired priest with the quivering lump of meat in his hands.

I had a million questions as the image formed in my mind.

Like, how big was this lump? Palm-sized? Big enough to fit in his hand? Or was it huge, like basketball-sized? Was it an enormous nugget of flesh carved out of the side of a huge animal like a dinosaur? Or was the flesh lump supposed to be a chunk of Jesus?

It must have been slick and bloody, right? Like something out of a horror movie. Or was it dried like jerky? Or perhaps worse, just a skin-covered blob? Any bones in it?

Further, what did the priest do with it?

Did he freak out?

Or did he just carry on as normal?

How did he continue the ritual of communion —
where everyone eats a bread wafer that symbolizes
Christ? His congregation would have been waiting to
eat the wafer. Did they see this? What did they do?

What if, when it was time for communion and I took
the wafer in my mouth, it turned into a lump of flesh in
my throat and I choked to death?

That seems like something God the psycho would
do.

The point here is that stories of religion are often
scary. More than the scariest horror movie.

But my family, we are a nice people, a friendly
people, a curious people.

My mother was kind to religious messengers.

When Jehovah Witness missionaries came to our
home, instead of slamming the door in their face as
most folks do, she would invite them in to discuss and
debate matters of religion.

Like me, she shared a fascination with the
philosophies people assemble as we all go through this
mysterious, terrifying and occasionally beautiful thing
called life.

She was open to hearing anyone's approach.

For her, this curiosity manifested as having an
earnest convo with Jehovah's Witnesses.

For me, this curiosity manifests as a compulsion to
read internet comments.

We are eager to learn other people's perspectives.

However, at the time as a wee teen, I didn't know
any of this.

All I knew was these two old ladies came to our
house and they had, let's say "a weird vibe." They were
strange. They were talking about end times and
punishment and fire from the sky and God's wrath, and

what little I overheard scared the crap out of me.

We were playing with our friends in the backyard — climbing trees, throwing a ball around, the usual kid stuff. But I was afraid for my mom's safety. I went inside and got my Boy Scout penknife, a multitool about as long as your finger with a blade among its many gadgets.

If these women came for my mom, I was armed and ready.

A friend noticed me sliding it into my back pocket.

"Why do you have a pen knife?" he asked.

Apparently, I was not the stealthy ninja assassin I had hoped to be.

"I don't," I said.

"I just saw you put it in your pocket."

That's where my memory fogs. I don't know how I explained it. We went back to playing and I had the knife ready. My mom never screamed for help.

After play when I went back inside. The ladies were gone.

Only a copy of "The Watchtower" magazine remained.

What is beautiful for some is horrifying for others.

That's why I'm still interested in other people's views.

Thanks, Mom!

34

ACRONYMS AND MNEMONICS

Whenever I need to quickly remember something, I convert it to an acronym.

When I wanted to use my time more meaningfully, I came up with STUD (Smart Time-Usage Daily.)

Being a stud and being mindful of how you use your time are not necessarily linked, but it still works. When I wake up, get ready for the day, look in the bathroom mirror I say "STUD."

It's a natural response. Just ask... well, just ask me.

Another one I devised is HEED. Which stands for Happy Each & Every Day. This seems a better option to use to start the day. It's a reminder to listen and a reminder to be mindful of your moods.

Wake up and HEED! Time is ticking.

That works better than STUD.

Let's take a moment to review the difference between acronyms and abbreviations.

An acronym spells an actual word, an abbreviation does not.

An acronym is something like we've discussed, STUD or HEED.

An abbreviation is just shorthand. Like XYZPDQYJIV (eXamine Your Zipper Pretty Darn Quick Your Junk Is Visible).

Acronyms are better, because as words, they can add to the memorability.

For example, a continual reminder that spells ALWAYS (Advance Love While Always You Smile.)

Contrast that with the famous acronym KISS: Keep It Simple, Stupid.

I'm not a fan of the KISS acronym because a lip lock has nothing to do with running an efficient process. Plus, it's unnecessarily mean. Keep It Simple, Silly, is better. But still, what does a peck on the cheek have to do with simplicity?

An acronym that reminds us to keep things simple would be better like this: SIMPLE = Suppress Irrelevant Motions, Promote Labor Efficiency. Okay, it's a little clunky but discussing simplicity with an acronym SIMPLE is better than KISS.

You say "KISS!" in a business meeting and there's no telling what might happen.

The recent horde of generative artificial intelligence tools are superb at acronym-making and brainstorming. For example, I teamed up with an AI bot and set it to work with this prompt: "Create several positive five-word daily advice phrases that spell DAILY." With minimal touch-up, here are my favorites.

1. Dream Always, Inspire Love, Yearn.
2. Discover Abilities, Inspire Leadership. Yes!
3. Don't Avoid, Invest Love, Yourself.
4. Direct Action, Impact Legacy, Yields-rewards.
5. Drive Ambitions, Invoke Laughter, Yeehaw!

Not bad, bot boy!

Anyway, while I've mentioned my criticisms about KISS, sometimes when the resulting word is a bit off kilter there's fun results. For example…

• TWERK = True Wisdom Eternally Rewards Kindness. I like the strange juxtaposition here of a ridiculous dance move where one makes one's buttocks jiggle, yet the word describing said jiggling stands for a profound call to kind action.

• STOP = Speed To Other Places. I use this when someone criticizes my driving. I explain that I thought that's what the STOP sign meant. This is best deployed when some goody-two-shoes in the passenger seat comments I didn't brake sufficiently. Hey, you ain't dead, stop complaining.

• TOILET = Times Of Intimacy, Loving Every Thing. Another profound meaning silly word mash-up. I used this one as advice to a newly married couple. "Now remember, you two lovebirds, TOILET." When I shared it with a bridesmaid, she loved it. No, she didn't, you say, she pretended to love it, she was just humoring you. If that's the case, then why was she on the reception dance floor screaming TOILET? Okay fine, you're right, she was drunk.

The greatest achievement of my acronym engineering (acro-neering?) was creating an acronym that helps one spell the weirdly-spelled word MNEMONIC. With one stroke, I created an acronym for mnemonic AND a mnemonic for mnemonic!

Here it is…

MNEMONIC: Maybe Now, Easily Memorizing One Noun Is Clear.

I don't think I'll ever top that. Unless you count this next one.

ACRONYM: A Concise Representation Of Nouns You Memorize.

That's enough, you say?

Did you perhaps mean, ENOUGH? End Now Or U Get Hit?

Okay.

I'll stop.

PROMISE. (Pledge Reliability Openly, Maintaining Integrity & Strong Effort.)

35

THE HIDDEN AGENDA OF STUPID TROUBLE

The late U.S. Representative John Lewis once made an inspirational statement about getting into "Good trouble." Here's what he said:

"Do not get lost in a sea of despair. Be hopeful, be optimistic. Our struggle is not the struggle of a day, a week, a month, or a year, it is the struggle of a lifetime. Never, ever be afraid to make some noise and get in good trouble, necessary trouble." Source: https://www.usatoday.com/story/news/politics/2020/07/18/rep-john-lewis-most-memorable-quotes-get-good-trouble/5464148002/

I love that quotation, that encouragement to be disobedient, but do so mindfully, intentionally.

He reminds us that when it is necessary to fight for justice, you may need to break some laws to make your point. That's okay. Just be smart about it.

You may need to trespass and carry a sign, get arrested to make your point. It's a lesson in civil disobedience. If you do it carefully, don't hurt anyone and break laws with a view toward protest, that's "Good trouble." In the fight for justice, it's necessary. If there's a law that says you cannot sit at a counter because of your skin color, sit there anyway and let them arrest you. Demonstrate the absurdity of the law.

If your elected officials insist on destroying the environment, go occupy their office until they are forced to speak with you.

You're breaking the law, but doing so non-violently. No one gets hurt and you make a statement. You will face consequences, but that's why it's good trouble. I am moved by Lewis' words and tried to live by them, as should every American.

However, I have a personal problem with it.

I don't mean a disagreement. I mean a problem in implementing it. I'm not good at it. I seem to be more skilled at getting into what I call "Stupid Trouble."

Meaning, I am not a natural talent at the traditional kind of rule-breaking that makes a statement, that noble civil disobedience backed by a concern for justice.

No.

The trouble I get into is often completely unnecessary. It's usually a violation of unwritten, or even unimagined norms.

I don't mean I defy norms to be a jerk. That's just being anti-social. Like holding a door open for someone close behind you. That's a norm. To defy that norm, you're either not paying attention (it happens) or if you do it on purpose, you're probably being jerk-ish.

Contrast jerkiness with my tendency to break the unwritten rules of conformity imposed by a society run by cold, cruel, profit-seeking hierarchies.

For instance, there's no specific rule against referring to the uptight, arrogant, mediocre VP of the company as "dude" in an email directly to her. And yet, that is the kind of trouble I get into. I'm casual, a bit silly by nature. When the VP returns from an important gathering, I'll email her and write simply, "Hey dude, how was your meeting?"

Her reply? One line. "Don't call me dude."

She later confessed to not knowing that dude was a casual term for a friend, demonstrating for the millionth time how out of touch she was. The story became legend around the office. Quote: You said that? To the VP?

For those of you out there who take her side and feel that it was inappropriate to be so casual with the VP, I will say, "You're probably right," just to make you go away.

But my true self will respond – silently or not – like this, "There now, that's a good little servant."

You see, in these troubled times, people vote for fascists while at the same wondering, "How do fascists come to power? Like in Germany in 1930s?"

Actually, it's far worse than that. First, we must consider if they wonder at all. But if they do, we find they wonder, "What's a fascist?" and a subset of these dim creatures secretly ask, "What's a Germany?"

But I'm straying off the point here.

What was the point?

Ah, yes. Stupid Trouble.

Stupid Trouble is the more flamboyant, artsy sibling of Good Trouble. Stupid Trouble is the screw-up, high-maintenance sibling to the buttoned-up, proper Good Trouble.

I do strange things and commit bizarre acts in the name of fun. This annoys people. I'm not sure why.

Why do they care?

That's the question I want them to think about. Why do they care if my silliness has no effect on them? Why does it annoy them so?

The answer they should arrive it is, if it doesn't bother me, I should not care about it. If they don't arrive at that conclusion they shall feel the pain of annoyance.

There exists in our society a sort of amateur police force, attempting to enforce compliance with these unwritten, arbitrary, unnecessary rules.

Maybe it's an evolutionary thing.

We have fancy gadgets, but as a society, we're still just a tribe of cave primates. The alpha doesn't like non-conformists because he wants full control. The rest of the tribe wants conformity because they fear the wrath of the alpha.

If you act a little off, the fearful non-alphas encourage you to stop drawing attention to yourself.

That is where good trouble comes in, but even more so, stupid trouble. Good trouble is obvious and intentional. Stupid trouble is fun and ridiculous. Both annoy those who get annoyed at a lack of control of others.

Good trouble is intentional. Stupid trouble is accidental.

Both have the positive effect of annoying those who seek to rule.

As a writer, it's my job to articulate. To put to words the many things we experience and feel so our brains can more fully grasp those ideas.

But for this one moment, I'll ditch the writer gig and grant myself a simple phrase for those who seek to control.

Fuck 'em all.

Let's have some fun. When possible, let's get in necessary, good trouble. The rest of the time, unnecessary, stupid trouble will do.

Goofing off at work is a way of defying this low-level corporate slave state we live in, where we must work very hard (or at least pretend to work very hard) to prevent the authorities from taking us away for not working hard enough.

Let's get in some stupid trouble.

36

DECODING THE EXTREMELY DIFFICULT TO UNDERSTAND DIFFERENCE BETWEEN "REPLY" AND "REPLY ALL"

All of the children from multiple families are packed into a car, driving home from some fun event at an amusement park or carnival or something.

The car is quiet.

Then suddenly, one kid remembers to thank the mom who is driving.

"Thank you, Mrs. Beanbutter!" this clever and polite child says.

Then all the other kids chime in. For a few moments after that one pioneer of appreciation, there follows a pop-pop-popping of thanks as every child expresses their gratitude.

"Thank you, Mrs. Beanbutter!"

"Thank you, Mrs. Beanbutter!"

"Thank you, Mrs. Beanbutter!"

This phenomenon is adorable when you see it in

children.

But it's super annoying when you experience it years later at your office job in the form of a reply-all email.

These digital echo chambers arise when everyone replies to everyone else unnecessarily. They usually begin with a "Welcome our new teammate!" or "Congratulate our teammate!" email.

It's fine to welcome someone, or congratulate someone, but does every recipient then need to "reply all?" Do those who are not congratulating — or the one being congratulated — need fifty copies of the same email? Do I need to be made aware of everyone saying thanks or congrats?

No.

I get that managers and corporate climbers want to maintain and/or bolster their brand as a team player. They want to appear friendly and welcoming regardless of the reality. It's an easy Brand You marketing tactic. These types don't want to thank or congratulate the person as much as they want to be seen doing so.

But casually irritating reply-all chains occur too often to be conscious. I think their cause is a soup of reflex, instinct, laziness, and conformity.

Are we alone in the universe?

Is there life after death?

Will people ever learn the difference between reply and reply all?

These are the mysteries of our existence.

It's a small complaint in the grand scheme of things. But it can have enormous consequences. Do an internet search for "email storm" (what this phenomenon is called) and you'll see true tales of out of control reply-alls crashing the servers of large companies.

I have dreams of a small software change: Whenever someone clicks reply all, the email app sends up a pop-up caution window to confirm their choice.

"You have hit REPLY ALL. Does your message only apply to the original sender? If yes, Use Reply. Is it ABSOLUTELY NECESSARY that your message be read by everyone on this email? If yes, use Reply All. Are you sure you want to send this message to everyone in the group? If it only applies to the original sender, it is better to use Reply."

There can be a check box "Don't ever show this warning again."

The button options would be Cancel, Continue with Reply All, Switch to Reply.

The default option would be Switch to Reply for fans of quick keys like me.

You're welcome, world.

But don't thank me… Oh no. You hit reply all!

37

NOTES FOR KING SOLOMON ON HIS SPLIT-THE-BABY DECISION

When I was an obnoxious teen, before I was the obnoxious adult I am today, I once got my parents with a prank.

I got them good. Real good.

Somehow one evening, our family of four were chatting and the biblical story of Solomon and the baby came up. I refer to the famous tale from the Bible, 1 Kings 3:16-28.

My younger brother hadn't heard of it.

"What's that?" he asked.

I, the elder, explained.

"There is a story in the Bible, where two women were arguing over who was the mother of a baby. They came before King Solomon…"

My parents were beaming, their pride glowing so strongly, I got radiation poisoning, or at least sunburn. The scene was Americana in its most imaginary glory: parents looking on with approval as their eldest son taught their youngest a story from the Bible.

You can see it as a Norman Rockwell style painting.

I continued the tale. My parents were quiet and still, not wanting to disturb this precious scene.

"Solomon said, fine, I'll cut the baby in half," I continued. "And one woman said, 'That works for me.' And the other woman said…"

I paused for a moment to build dramatic anticipation. My parents leaned closer.

"And the other woman said, 'Yeah I'm good with that, too.'"

My parents howled.

They absolutely roared in protest.

I cackled evilly.

My brother was confused.

"What's happening?"

"Nooooo!" my parents wailed, surely sounding a lot like people in a city that God decided to torch because someone there had too much sex.

"He's telling it wrong!"

After I finished my evil laughter, I told my younger bro the real story.

"Solomon said let's split the baby. One woman said, okay that's fine and the other said no, let her have the child. And Solomon gave the baby to the woman against cutting the child. His reasoning was that a mother would never want to harm her child. Plus, chances were good that the baby would be in better shape with the woman who insisted he stay whole."

My parents appreciated that I knew the actual tale. They did NOT appreciate my remix.

But if they didn't like that, then they definitely won't like this next part, where I call into question Solomon's judgment. Or at least question this nifty bit of kingly propaganda.

See, the story of Solomon and the baby is a nice story, but it has always left me uneasy.

It's all too clean. That sets off warning bells for me.

You can see similar stories like this online all the time: obviously made-up tales that fit together too perfectly to exist in the messy, chaotic real world. These goofball anecdotes always happen to be a concise and perfect illustration of whatever agenda the teller supports. They often star an innocent child.

For example, some general issue politician might post this: "My two-year-old son came up to me to said, 'Daddy, why do we tax rich people? Aren't rich people the ones who invest and create most of the jobs?'"

Obviously false, obviously intended to push an agenda. The goal is to make lower taxes for the rich seem so obvious that even a child would understand.

Here's another example I just made up, but that probably would be used in earnest: "A veteran came up to me in tears. He said that he fought for the right for healthcare conglomerates to charge you out the ass."

Or whatever.

Over the years I've become very skeptical of stories with neat conclusions. Life is so random, few events have a clean moral lesson at any point.

Another red flag for bogusness is the presence of karma.

In real life, karma is a happy accident. In most cases, people getting what they deserve is often a convoluted sloppy mess. Or they don't notice they got what they deserved based on their own choices and actions, or, as a last defense, even if they get what they deserve, and they notice it, they still blame the wrong culprit anyway.

The story of Solomon and the baby has all those warning signs of a lie: it's all too neat, too clean, and has the presence of obvious karma.

The whole tale is incomplete.

We never find out more detail about why the woman agreed to cut the baby in half.

We never get to investigate, to speak with her and ask, "Are you serious? You would really let him cut the baby in half? Like, literally slice him in half. With a sword. For reals?"

I feel we're only getting a part of the story. Like a child that only exists from the waist up. Or waist down. Ah, hell, I say waist-up. Keep the head. I'm a child half-full kind of guy.

Anyway, that uncertainty, that complete incomprehensible horror at someone else's decisions — that's what it feels like to disagree strongly with someone. And I feel it's better we learn to understand disagreements before make sweeping assumptions and kingly judgments about people's motivations.

People have reasons.

You might not like the reasons, you might not agree with the thought process, and their process might be self-contradictory, but they have a reason. You just need to ask.

But Solomon never asks.

He simply renders his judgment, and everyone talks about how great he is.

I've always wanted to know more about the woman who agreed to cut the baby in half. We need to know more about her. Empathy is putting yourself in someone else's heart. There are many reasons why a woman might agree to split the baby.

WHAT? No, I'm not advocating for diced infant, unless of course said baby is sitting behind me on an airplane and won't stop kicking my seat. I'm just saying there are reasons a mother might agree to slicing up her own child.

1. Maybe the woman is succumbing to mental illness and needs help.
2. Maybe the child is a product of an abusive relationship — and she can't bear the thought of his existence.
3. Maybe she's so frustrated that someone would try to steal her child, that she goes into that common human desperation mode: if I can't have my way, no one will.
4. Maybe she knows the child is destined for a life of slavery and she wishes to spare him.
5. Maybe she was calling Solomon's bluff and agreeing with his split-the-baby proposal to kiss his ass, in the hopes that by agreeing, she'll win his favor.
6. Maybe she knows that to disagree with the king is a death sentence.
7. Maybe the other woman, who said "Don't split the baby!" had heard of this trick before and she knew what to say to win the trial.

I'm a philosopher myself, so no shade for Solomon. He did the best with what he had. He had no witnesses, no security camera footage, no DNA testing, and there were surely other kingly duties on his agenda for the day.

He did well (generous of me to give him a passing grade, eh?) and it's never foolish to wonder if I'm wasting my time by over-thinking a fable.

But I think humans err more often by oversimplifying than overcomplicating.

Let's pretend I'm on to something.

Maybe Solomon should have asked more questions, given the lady help, and inquired about her living conditions. Why are they living in such a way that someone can steal another's baby and it's not clear who the child's mother is? Maybe he should have asked about all that, and proposed a solution, being king and all.

We just don't know the things people go through.

When they are acting strange, instead of making assumptions, it's better to wonder why.

38

GOOD OMENS, BAD DREAMS, DOG POOP

There is an old saying, what some would call "an old wives' tale" before that phrase became punishable by public lashing.

The idea goes like this: "When you have a bad dream, that means you'll have good luck."

Another variation is "When you dream you're dying, you'll have good luck."

I've always wondered where these began. Who came up with these rules?

Some superstitions and myths have an origin story in common sense or at least good advice.

For example, "Don't walk under a ladder. It's bad luck." Well, maybe. It's also common sense because something on the ladder, or the person on it, or something the person on the ladder is holding, might drop and gonk you on the head.

"Don't break a mirror, it's seven years bad luck." That's another one that seems like it could have

144

originated when servants were moving expensive items back when. The mirror was fragile, rare, and expensive. To break it would earn a whipping by the master. The consequences were real, the threat of seven years bad luck was made up to terrify you cautious.

But back to this specific one: "When you have a bad dream, that means you'll have good luck."

Did someone track that and prove it with data? Seems doubtful.

How could one compare a day that starts with a terrifying dream to the percentage of waking success? It sounds like someone just made it up.

I suspect someone did, and I know who that someone is.

Mothers, across the world.

Let's imagine it.

A child screams in the darkness of night.

The harried mother rushes to their bedside, "What's wrong?"

"I had a scary dream."

"Oh no, honey, it's not real. You're okay."

"I can't go back to sleep."

"Yes, you can."

"No, I can't."

"But I have to work in a few hours. Go back to sleep."

"I'm scared I'll have another nightmare. I dreamed I died."

Mom sees the glow of the rising sun, valuable sleep slipping away. Desperately, she does some quick brainstorming.

"Bad dreams mean you're going to have good luck," she says.

The child stops sobbing. "They do?"

Mom, realizing she's getting somewhere, confirms it.

"Yes, dear. They do."

And there you go. A myth is born.

I came to this theory when something similar happened to me.

I was the role of the mother trying to comfort someone.

I can't recall the exact circumstances, but we were all dressed up. It was probably a wedding or something and someone stepped in dog poop or spilled something on their nice dress.

They became annoyed and frantic when they noticed the mess, cursing fate.

As everyone assisted in the cleaning, the victim became more stressed. The worry was pushing them into a panic spiral, ruining the joyful day.

So, I just made something up.

"Oh, um, hey, I heard that's a sign of good luck."

Later I realized I should have added some glitter like, "My grandmother always said…" or "Back in the old country…" etc.

The claim took the sting out of the misfortune. A few people chuckled, knowing that I was lying. But even a lie can help. It prevents the victim from disappearing into a philosophical vortex about the uncaring nature of our universe.

The victim didn't exactly say, "I'll have good luck, you say? Well then, I shan't get too upset." But they were distracted and the bad vibes passed.

As I said, my memory is hazy.

Our world is random and often cruel. But if you tell someone they're going to have good luck at some point in the future, they feel empowered to push through the messy present.

So go ahead and lie to your friends and loved ones to manipulate them.

It's worked for religion.

39

THE VALUE OF LIES IN CHURCH

Let me set the scene here for those who weren't raised
Roman Catholic, as I was.

Eventually you reach a point in Catholic
indoctrination where you go through a ritual called
"Confirmation." This is a ceremony where you swear
your allegiance to the Church for the rest of your life.

There are similar rituals in other religions. I think the
Bar-Bat-Mitzvah stuff in Judaism is close, but I don't
know much about that or care to do a few seconds of
an online search right now, so I'll just mention it and
move on.

After enduring boring training at the church during
my schooling years, I was eventually ready to be capital-
C Confirmed.

This was extremely bad news.

I had doubts. As a young person in his late teens, I
didn't feel ready to commit to anything for my entire
life. I didn't want to choose a career, or join the military,
or sign over my soul to a church. Yet at that age, the

pressure to commit was everywhere. All kinds of institutions were fighting for the fresh meat. They target the young to bring into their fold. All these powerful groups were in my face, trying to recruit me for the rest of my life.

In addition to that pressure, what made the impending ritual much more stressful was that during this phase of my romantic youth, I was vehemently opposed to lying.

Totally against it. Zealously so.

I had heard a quote: "None but cowards lie." And I loved it. I did not want to be a coward, so I swore I would not lie. Every day I did my best. I vowed that if I ever said "I promise" I would not betray that bond. Too many people are too casual with their oaths, they don't follow through, and soon enough their words mean nothing.

I wanted my words to mean something.

These two ideas were on a collision course: Obligatory Religious Commitment and A Refusal to Lie.

I spoke to a friend who went through Confirmation ritual about my concerns.

He laughed at my anxiety, at my desire to stay true and avoid confirming myself to the Catholic Church.

"I just lied," he said. "Because the entire thing was a farce."

I envied his casual approach.

As a mature adult, I see the value that a well-placed, simple lie can provide. Done right, lying is a real time-saver and a necessary tool for social survival. Plus, it helps get you hired.

But as a militant youth, I refused.

If I was fine with my words meaning little, there would be no story here.

But as I was, this upcoming public Confirmation was

a source of terror.

If I gave my word, in God's home, to God and everyone, then I was locked in. For life. Because one thing I didn't do was lie. I didn't and I wouldn't. But people would be watching me in a public ceremony, they would wait for me to verbally confirm my soul.

I had to think of something. Somehow, I had to escape.

The problem tormented me for weeks.

I considered dropping out of the whole ritual but I didn't know if that was an option. I didn't want to upset my parents either, as all this ceremonial stuff meant a lot to them. I was trapped, flailing about in a cage sliding toward a pit of lava.

No answers arrived. Soon I was in the church for the day of the ceremony, still with no solution.

We were in a line. Dozens of us teens arrayed next to an adult we respected — not a parent but other adult member of the church — who would be present to witness us become fully Catholic. I had chosen the father of a high school friend who was a good man, and a nice guy.

I thought about faking an illness or pretending to faint. I considered running out of the church but I didn't want to do anything embarrassing or cause drama.

My family and our church kin were all around, all smiling and supportive.

They were kind people. I had to somehow get through this, without committing, and without causing stress to these well-meaning folk whom I admired.

Time was running out.

The first kid went up.

The priest said some words. I don't recall what they were but something like, "Do you confirm your life to the Catholic Church?"

In the hard, cold chamber of polished wood and marble, all definition of the sound was lost, so it sounded like the priest asked, "Oo oo oh eh oh ah ot ah ah eh uh?"

Then teen then mumbled the response we had memorized, something like "Yes I do, father. I confirm." Which, thanks to the acoustics, sounded like "Eh ah ooh ah eh oh eh."

The priest made some gestures, said some other Ah Eh Ooh Oh Uh stuff, and the teen was turned away. A newly-minted lifelong Roman Catholic walked down the aisle.

The line moved forward.

The ritual of the call and response continued. The line chunked forward. And again. And again. A reliable conveyer belt of efficiency was shipping souls to the Lord in bulk.

The whole time, my mind was frantic, absolutely buzzing, trying to figure out how I could get through this without giving my word.

"Oo oo oh eh oh ah ot ah ah eh uh?"

"Eh ah ooh ah eh oh eh."

"Oh ah ah eh eh ah."

And suddenly there I was, at the front of the line. Time's up.

The priest said something, and even just an arm's length away, in the echo chamber of the open area, it sounded like that mumbling, vowel-heavy speech.

"Oo oo oh eh oh ah ot ah ah eh uh?"

And it came to me. Like divine intervention.

The solution was there.

I bowed my head, and instead of saying, "Yes, I do, father, I confirm."

I literally said this: "Eh ah ooh ah eh oh eh."

I mimicked the sounds of the words, but I didn't say them. No commitment.

Also, not a lie.

I looked up.

The priest stared at me. Hesitated.

Our eyes met.

He paused.

After a few moments, he continued pausing.

It was a pause so wide, you could march all the children who had been molested by priests through it.

He knows!

I was panicking.

He figured it out! I'm doomed.

He's going to make me repeat it more clearly, and if he does that, I'm done for. Since I don't lie, I will have committed my life to this centuries-old institution that I don't trust.

Disaster.

My life will be over before it's begun.

I'm busted.

Wait!

Maybe, just maybe, in the thoughts behind the priest's eyes, maybe he thinks I have a speech impediment or something.

No! He knows! He suspects something is amiss.

He can see into my soul.

Why is he taking so long?

He didn't take this long with the others!

He wants a repeat. No!

No, please God, no!

He's going to make me do it again! He'll have me repeat my response clearly!

Then his eyes softened, and a weariness stole across his face. A giant line stretched out behind me, and there were so many others to confirm. So many more to bring in.

Best to keep the line moving, he thought.

He raised his hand, made the sign of the cross.

"Oh ah ah eh eh ah," he said, and sent me away.

As I turned and walked away from the altar, my heart soared. It was a religious experience. Or its opposite.

I left the church that day, physically and spiritually. Even better, I didn't lie before God, for I had said no words.

Victory!

Looking back, I recall an old playground trick. If you crossed your fingers when you told a lie, then it was okay to say something false. It was up to the listener to keep an eye on your hand.

I could have just done that.

I could have done a bunch of things, but I like what I did.

Our culture demands children to commit to things before they're ready.

Eventually they just learn to lie, to not take commitment seriously.

Maybe that's why so many who call themselves Christian act in horrifically un-Christ-like ways. A lifetime of developing casual duplicity surely doesn't help.

Whether it's committing to a country, to a church, to an army, or to a college – that is a lot of pressure.

Teens are trying to be sincere. But the world of adults demonstrates you don't have to bother with that nonsense. Just lie all the time, break your word and move on. Learn to do it. You get used to it. It's fine.

Even me, of course.

I'm no longer an anti-lying zealot.

Were I in the Confirmation situation again as an adult, I would just lie.

Like my friend said, the whole thing was a farce, just say what they want even if you don't mean it. Be done and move on.

I could easily do that now.

And I don't know if that's good or bad.

40

ALL HAIL SASQUATCH, ZEN MASTER OF CRYPTIDS

Consider the cryptids, creatures of myth.

Most have a purpose loosely based on Puritan ethics. They snatch babies from bad mommies. They devour disobedient children. They drink the blood of unguarded innocents and leave them to die in horror.

For clarity, we're still talking cryptids, not health insurance, but I understand any confusion.

Let's focus on one specific cryptid: Sasquatch.

He's an exception to this mythical enforcer of polite society's manners.

He runs around and is seen.

He doesn't interfere with human lives or threaten violence for ignoring religious dogma.

His lone goal appears to be this: he wants to be left alone.

I suppose we could say the same about the Loch Ness Monster. But I believe Nessie has been rumored to pilfer livestock sometimes. That's annoying. You got to bed having counted your 252 sheep, awake the next day, start the count again, but all the damn sheep keep moving around, so you put them in the pen and count them as they exit the gate. But some won't exit, or they turn around and go back, leaving you to wonder how such unruly willful creatures that became symbols of human conformity but never mind that pay attention because now you have to start counting again and it takes all damn day and then by the time you're done you've only counted 251 sheep. You're pretty sure you got the count right so that can only mean…

Curse you, Nessie!

Quetzalcoatl (forgive me, spell check) devours humans.

Werewolves maim people.

Witches and warlocks kill your crops.

Sasquatch simply is.

And that appears to be good enough for him. He just wants to be.

He values his privacy. A lot. Imagine Sasquatch's horror if he read the Terms and Conditions of a social media website and all that legalese that essentially says, "Don't expect any real privacy if you use this site."

He'd be horrified.

Wandering, exploration, and simply relaxing are the keys to a peaceful, enjoyable life. But those things are forbidden in a world run by capitalism.

You can't just be. You must fit somewhere in the economic machine. You must be "useful." You must have a job title, and that role must be fulfilled, and if it isn't? Well then you just don't really exist or you're not living up to what you should be doing, etc.

Serve the market or die.

But not Sasquatch! He doesn't care.

He's doing it right. He keeps to himself and that

seems just fine with him. That's why we never see him, or when we do, he's in the distance, running away.

For all of us living under the pressure of capitalism, ask yourself, why does a cryptid have rights I don't?

Why must I have a brand, a mission statement, an objective, a website with a call-to-action button that sends me more work?

Why do I have to be CEO of Brand Me?

Why do I have to do a bunch of busy crap to fill out my resume?

Answer: I don't. None of us do.

Sasquatch doesn't.

He just is, and that's good enough. Capitalism be damned.

Thank you, Sasquatch, you're an inspiration.

41

MY SPOKESPERSON, MY HERO

I'm always impressed by spokespeople.

These are the brave souls who take all the questions and complaints from the public, and make their employer — an individual, a company, an athlete, a government agency, whatever — sound like their client never made a mistake ever. And if it appears they made a mistake, well then, you foolish clown, you're the one who's mistaken.

No matter what incoherent babbling nonsense the president says, no matter how many times he staggers across a stage looking like he's searching for the pudding buffet whilst blindfolded and with a full adult diaper, his spokesperson will describe him as a fitness superstar, ready to lead high-intensity aerobics classes for the next eight hours while discussing the finer legal points of international trade.

And if you disagree, you're worse than the scum of the Earth, you're the scum of Uranus.

A company can drop chemical waste into a town's

drinking water, causing all its residents to have explosive diarrhea for a month, but the spokesperson will come out and tell those people they should be thankful.

The company wasn't careless, it was just a sad accident.

The company is the real victim here.

It all makes me wish I had a spokesperson.

I could use someone who would go out and handle all the questions to explain away the dumb stuff I do. Or, even better, make it sound like the dumb stuff I did was intentional and noble. Ever better than that, make it sound like anyone questioning my motives or actions is really the villain. Here's a sample transcript.

MY SPOKESPERSON (MSP): Good afternoon, everyone. We have time for a few questions.
REPORTER: At oh four hundred hours yesterday morning, Larry mixed his marijuana gummies with rum and several microwaved spicy burritos. He then vomited on the floor.
MSP: That information is disputed.
REPORTER: But we have it on video.
MSP: (Contemptuous sigh) While it is true that he vomited, it has not been determined that the cause was drinking too much.
REPORTER: You're saying he may have been sick? Had the flu?
MSP: I'm saying there are many other possible reasons. And for the record, I do not subscribe to your implication that his conduct was irresponsible. Next question.
OTHER REPORTER: Don't you feel that it was childish for Larry to play Call of Duty on Xbox for seven hours straight on the day of his wedding anniversary?

MSP: Larry works very hard and he's entitled to some relaxation. As are we all.

OTHER REPORTER: But this was a wedding anniversary. It's not as if he didn't know the date in advance.

MSP: I believe I've addressed those concerns adequately. Next question.

REPORTER: Larry was napping when he was supposed to be working.

MSP: That hasn't been confirmed.

REPORTER: There are multiple sources saying it's true.

MSP: That's all the time we have.

42

THE LATER YEARS OF THE KID WHO YELLED AT THE EMPEROR

One of my favorite stories of all time is the Emperor's New Clothes by Hans Christian Andersen.

It's a great lesson in conformity, Groupthink, and speaking up when everyone else is silent.

For those who don't know, the fable goes like this: some dudes come to town and tell the emperor that they've got cool new clothes for him. In fact, they don't have anything, but they lavish him with praise as he stands there naked. They're so good with the compliments that the emperor decides to strut through the streets with his new "clothes" which don't exist.

The Emperor goes walking through the streets naked, and all the adults, having learned from a life of oppression that they should conform, all gasp in awe at the clothes that are not there. They cheer obediently and rave about the fine garments.

Only a little child, who isn't yet indoctrinated, yells out, "But he's naked!" Or something like that.

The crowd is shocked and stunned but quickly recovers.

The end.

I like this story because it reinforces the obvious fact that much of being famous and rich is pretending that something that is mediocre (or even non-existent) is really great.

It could be a product, a cultural item, or even a spouse. Underserved praise comes in many forms, but I think in the form of modern art it's the most insulting.

My rule is this: If the art doesn't make you say 'Wow!' then it's not art. If the art is something you could replicate with minimal effort, then the art sucks.

A banana taped to a wall is not art. A photo of a crucifix in a glass of urine is not art. A single stripe down a canvas is not art. And so on.

Sometimes I just want to say to a critic, "It's okay to admit this sucks."

Be it a book called a classic, a famous painting, a hot new movie, or whatever.

But I think once you become a paid reviewer, you can get a ton of free crap if you praise anything. You become part of a network. Your publisher needs help selling other books, so you say, "Sure, I'll gush about that other book, even though I've never read it."

We need more voices like the kid in the Emperor's new clothes.

We need more people who say, "That's not great. Actually, it kind of stinks."

Where are those kids today?

I suspect they're living inside all of us.

We just need to let them yell out.

43

MOMS! AND KIDS!

In our dangerous world, we must always look for
warning signs and red flags. Avoiding hazards involves
at its core being aware of atmospheric signals. Not just
what you can see, not just the words you hear, but the
tones in which those words are spoken.

Notice the small but meaningful difference in how a
woman announces she has given birth.

If she casually mentions she has children, and she
says something like "I'm a mother, these are my kids,"
you should be okay. This is a normal person.

But if a woman says, "I'm a MOM!" and she says it
in all capitals, and lands on the word "Mom" with all
the righteousness of a miserable elderly person
overcharged a nickel, then you need to be alert.

Let me clarify.

Most moms are cool. They had a kid or kids, and
they don't think they're more special than anyone else.

But MOMs are not cool. To them, their act of giving
birth is the best birth that ever was or will be. They

enacted the will of God, fulfilled the purpose of humanity, defeated the terrorists, upheld the glory of our nation and said nation's favored ethnicities — all with one action: having a child.

If I had any courage (which I don't) I'd respond with something like, "Congrats. You have a functioning uterus. You know else has a functioning uterus? Five million rats."

Technically speaking, I do not know the specific stats on rat biology or reproduction.

The point is to take the MOM down a peg. Because they want to be on the highest peg. Higher than you and everyone else. The world is for the use of their spawn and their spawn alone.

MOMs are different than your standard mother.

MOMs are best avoided. They are identical to the eugenics-lite folks on cable news who imply (or often just say) that the USA needs to have more white babies.

MOMs are the ones who feel it's your responsibility to be as moved by their birthing as they are. And they feel the mere act of giving birth entitles them and their children to do as they please, every other single person in the world will just have to deal with it.

I'm especially disgusted by the way MOMs treat women who don't have children.

MOMs assume a woman either chose not to have children and is a monster, or due to some biological issue, couldn't have children and is miserable about their life every day.

I have often heard MOMs say things like this to women without children: "Oh you don't know love until you've had your own child."

The ignorance and intended cruelty, as well as the admission in such statements, is staggering. MOMs are women who obviously don't like being a mom, but since they are one, they behave in ways clearly designed to convince themselves that they love it.

But they did it to themselves, which probably makes them even more miserable. Motherhood is great, sure, but you know, it's also voluntary. (At least in the blue states.)

Here's another anecdote.

We went out for lunch one day. For some stupid reason, despite the restaurant being almost empty, the host sat us, a couple with no kids, adjacent to a booth with three rowdy kids and one woman.

Their MOM, as we would soon find out.

She could also have been their kidnapper or human trafficker. But these kids were so annoying, no kidnapper would have wanted them. No sane person would pay for these brats.

We were in the booth for a few minutes, the children kicking and screaming and running up and down the aisle. When the server came back, we quietly asked, "Can we move to another table?"

Of course, she said brightly. We moved down the aisle several booths away.

It was all very discreet.

We simply moved.

No problem.

Oops. Wait.

MOM has a problem.

The rowdy kids were running around and ventured all the way down past our new table. MOM was in pursuit, and that's when she noticed we had moved.

"You don't have kids, do you?" she asked. It sounded like a question but was more an accusation.

I didn't like her tone, so I ignored her, scanning the menu.

My wife, however, answered, sharing some counter-snippy words.

The woman gathered her mobile turds and marched back to the booth, where she went about continuing to hate her life.

My peace-loving hippie wife recalls the moment and says that she wanted to fight that woman. This is shocking because she never wants to fight anyone. Fortunately, there were no hands thrown. No five-minute hockey penalty.

Let's review the situation.

We didn't do anything but move. We didn't say a word. And yet MOM marched down the aisle and made a point to slyly judge us.

"You obviously don't have children," she said. But she meant, "So you obviously can't experience this joy. You don't have kids so you can't possibly understand how impossible it is to control them."

No. We don't have kids.

But if you want to get into it, there are people who do and they don't let their spawn run wild, then get snarky with people who quietly request not to be seated near such shit parenting.

How ya like me now?

Kids can be wonderful.

Watching my niece grow and being her favorite uncle has been one of the joys of my life.

But I don't think I'm special because of it.

Because you know who else was an uncle to their niece?

That's right.

Five million rats.

44

I DON'T WANT TO CIVIL WAR
WITH YOU, BRO

There's a certain type of American cryptid, usually male, who becomes sexually aroused at the idea of a second American Civil War.

Anyone who wants war has never been in one or they're psychotic.

But part of America's brand is casual cruelty, so it all fits.

Even so, I'm old enough to recall a time when war was considered bad. People agreed on that. War required our full attention — to end it as quickly as possible.

Now war is simply the white noise of the American empire, a background hiss no one notices unless you take a moment to think about it. Or review how much of our tax money is going to support it, to the benefit of only those who are selling the weapons.

Or worse, you're one of the unlucky families who loses a loved one in some skirmish somewhere in the world, announced to the rest of us Americans as, "Three servicemembers were killed in (COUNTRY) today."

Causing us to wonder, "We have troops there? But why?"

Those questions are never answered. The news promptly moves on. The white noise continues.

Many people are big fans of President Lincoln and how he preserved The Union, but I think maybe he made a mistake.

Was it wise to go that hard just to keep Alabama? Or Mississippi?

Ever since the Civil War they've been crying to get out.

I say let 'em go.

Let's imagine the young United States of the early 1860s as a party. A small clique called the Confederates is annoying everyone, acting like jerks, sitting in the corner whining, "This party sucks."

When that happens in real life, you and your friends bounce 'em.

"You don't like it, get out," you say.

Or, more likely, they just leave.

You don't force them to stay. You don't — as they exit — grab them and drag them back.

Who wants miserable people at a party?

Their ejection should NOT play out like this:

You say, "Hey, you guys are jerks."

They say, "Oh you think we're jerks, huh? Well then, we'll just leave."

"No. You have to stay."

"But you think we're jerks. We don't like you either. We want to leave."

"No. You have to stay AND you have to stop being jerks."

"But we want to keep being jerks."

"You have to behave how I want. And you have to stay."

"Oh yeah?"

(Big fight begins.)

Assume you win the big fight and you've tied the party-poopers to chairs or something. Now they're enraged and motivated to do anything they can with the goal of sabotaging the whole gathering.

Foolish, right?

Yet metaphorically speaking, that's exactly what Old Abe and the United States did and how the former Confederate states have reacted ever since.

Now some may be crying, "But the North went to war to stop slavery!"

I'm skeptical.

Yes, it's true that the South wanted to preserve slavery. Confederate mythology says the South just wanted to be free from the bullying Federal Government. But during recent years as Confederate monuments and flags have been officially taken down several decades late, we've reviewed the history. The leaders of the Confederacy were clear: they wanted to keep slaves.

Where I'm skeptical is the implication that the North fought the war solely to eliminate slavery. I have a hard time believing rich white men in the North pushed to attack the Southern states solely out of moral concern for poor black individuals.

I think they ran the same old play from the same old playbook. They wanted the land and the resources, they wanted money and power, but they emphasized the moral argument in their justifications for war. Being anti-slavery was convenient to the Northern war-makers in that it was morally correct.

It's a political tactic so old and obvious it makes me yawn to repeat it. They took the moral high ground because it aligned with their desired land-grab.

I could be wrong. You historians go debate amongst yourselves.

What I do know is that there was a fight, the miserable people stayed at the party, were forced to change their behavior, and they've been complaining, still wanting out, and trying to sabotage the gathering ever since.

What makes this situation weirder are all these bits of land that want in.

Most are called "Territories."

Puerto Rico, Guam, The Virgin Islands, American Samoa, and a whole bunch more I don't feel like looking up right now are absolutely begging to get into the United States. One of them is even the capital of the whole place, Washington, D.C.!

When you summarize it, the foolishness of it all jumps out –

1. We have the Confederate states begging to be let out, but we won't let them out.
2. We have some territories begging to be let in, but we won't let them in.

Isn't it time we let the ones who want out, out — and let the ones who want in, in?

Though I usually pick on Alabama and Mississippi for their atrocious civil rights history, my personal choice for the first to go is the always-talking-tough-about-freedom but rarely-delivering state of Texas.

Hey Texas! Yer outta here! Good luck with that privatized power grid! If Mexico wants to take you back, well, have fun! We forgot the Alamo!

Welcome, Puerto Rico.

One wants out, the other wants in, it's a no-brainer. Why all the fighting to resist this obvious move?

Trade Texas for Puerto Rico. Everyone gets their flags confused anyway. And speaking of flags, we don't have to change the USA's if we do one-for-one trades like this.

At this point having the USA flag with something other than 50 stars seems like a crime against nature. So let's move with baby steps. One for one.

No need for fighting. Trade the most annoying Confederate states for the American Empire's territories.

Everyone's happy. No flag redesign needed. Done and done.

When the Booting Starts the Shooting Starts

There's another thing that those horny for a second Civil War don't get. They think that because they all go to the gun range and run around the forest terrorizing deer that they are a lethal fighting force.

While they're preparing, they imagine we Yankees are buying overpriced coffee, wearing dresses, and having raunchy gay sex in front of children.

Meanwhile, they can't wait to kill us. It's kind of weird to fantasize out loud about murdering your neighbors, but I'm off track.

The point is, Civil War Two hopefuls believe Southerners, as a whole and on average, are better at firearms and therefore, they'd win the Civil War.

But that was the same situation in the first civil war. The South (so I'm told – and when has history ever lied?) had the greater military strategists, better soldiers, and better generals.

They lost.

This is what the Civil War Two fantasy role players don't seem to get: war isn't a matter of skill.

It doesn't matter if you have the guns. It doesn't matter if you have good generals.

Wars are won by money just like sports championships, but there's no salary cap in war. You can borrow and spend, borrow and spend. Put your French and Prussian and German mercs on the credit card until your opponent can't keep up, and then you win.

Then for the rest of your existence you're paying back the debt, but at least you're not dead.

War is won by money and that's why the South would lose again. With few exceptions, the northern states are richer.

The Confederacy is stuck with the USA.

Their final revenge should be to get the most corrupt, ethics-free, immoral representatives into the federal government and make life hell for everyone.

I don't know why they want a rematch.

Seems they won the first time.

45

DEATH AND/OR HOMICIDE WHILE PLAYING "THE PENIS GAME"

What exactly is "The Penis Game?"

This is a sport developed by my niece and her friends while at grade school. Variations of it likely exist worldwide in other forms, but what follows are the basic rules.

The game is best played on a bus. Each player takes a turn yelling the word "Penis!" as loud as possible. Whoever yells the loudest wins.

That's the game.

When our niece explained she and her classmates were playing this fun contest, my wife and I, being the aunt and uncle we are, didn't say "You shouldn't do that, it's immature."

Instead, we asked, "Who won?"

Our niece informed us the victor was her friend. "Sarah."

Ha! Imagine that! One of her fellow girl classmates defeated all the boys at The Penis Game.

A victory for equality, no doubt. I think.

Now, several years later, the niece is a first-year student at university. While she was back for her winter break, I was driving, taking her along to run some errands.

I guess she was overtaken by nostalgia and suggested we play The Penis Game, with the variation that we wouldn't just compete on volume, but how much we could attract the attention of innocent pedestrians.

Being a mature adult, I agreed to the contest.

We were driving along, looking for targets.

Then suddenly she started screaming.

Then suddenly I started screaming.

But we weren't screaming, "Penis!"

We both were shouting in horror.

Fortunately, no one was hurt. The danger was over as quickly as it had passed.

What had happened?

I ran a red light.

Not just any red light. The main intersection in town.

Though each cross street was filled with cars wanting to get from point A to point B, none were quick on the pedal as we rocketed through the forbidden intersection.

I was goddamned embarrassed.

What awful result could have been?

You see officer, I killed that family yes, but it's all very innocent. I'm sure you'll understand. I was playing The Penis Game with my teenaged niece.

Long ago, as a dumb teen, I had been speeding for fun and caused a serious accident.

Every day since, I thank all the gods, demons, demigods, tech execs, and crypto-con-men that exist that no one was hurt. The car was totaled but no one was injured.

It was a miracle. A genuine miracle.

Had I learned nothing?

It would seem so.

Sometimes the things I write and share seem like a public confessional.

This is one of those times.

46

ARLO: ONE ODD CAT

Hello dear reader. Thank you for taking this journey as we relive the laughs and head-shaking moments getting to know one of the strangest domestic cats I've ever lived with.

I want to get something out of the way first.

Arlo has passed on.

He lived a great life, a long life full of adventure and love, but he is now deceased.

What?!

Why would I tell you this to start? Why start with a bummer?

Because I don't want you to hear the end of Arlo's story and go away sad. As you'll soon learn, every day I knew him was an extra day he might not have had. There are too many books and movies out there that tell the stories of wonderful animals, then the animals die at the end, leaving their new friends a blubbering mess.

Rather than score cheap emotional points, I'm telling you now. He is no longer with us, physically. And of course that makes me sad, but I'm also thankful I got to know him, live with him, and go nuts chasing after him, organizing the chaos in his wake, and paying for his astronomical veterinary hospital bills.

I'm grateful he got well over a decade in bonus years.

As with all whom we love, his legacy lives on in silly tales, in aggravating memories, and stories of adventure.

I like to say, "The body is gone, but the legend lives on."

In my life, there's been many cats, but none quite as bizarre as Arlo. I can't say he was my favorite cat because there were times he was a downright irritating jerk.

Of course I love all my cats, I dare not do otherwise, but most of their stories don't translate so easily into compelling reading. Arlo was one of those big personalities who always did things in a bizarre way, ready-made for sharing.

"Remember the time Arlo did….?"

For example, most cats I've lived with have been gentle strays, staying for a while, then permanently.

Or they've been adopted from a shelter, or from someone who, for whatever reason, couldn't care for the cat any longer.

None, however, entered my life by lying in the street, motionless.

I love the other cats, but Arlo had showmanship.

Like any good performer, he made a big entrance.

The Day We Met

"This cat is either dead or sleeping in a really bad place," I said to myself.

I could see him from a distance.

He was curled up inches from the curb, in the road near the base of a tree. Why would a cat sleep there?

Was the black top warm? Had he just said, Aw heck, I'm tired, this will do... in the worst possible spot?

More likely, he was dead.

If he was sleeping, a driver who didn't see him would surely hit him.

I swerved to the side of the lonely suburban road.

I pulled alongside the curled-up ball of black fur, and beeped the horn, hoping to wake this eccentric fellow. I wanted to scare him away to a better nap spot or, know for certain if he was gone.

I hadn't thought of the third option: he was alive — but severely wounded.

He looked up at me, dark blood caked in the fur under his chin, his meow silent through my closed passenger window.

As I am prone to do in a crisis, I immediately panicked.

I put the car in park and jumped out, talking to myself out loud.

"Oh my god. Oh my god."

My heart rattled.

I gently lifted him, trying to keep his head and neck in alignment so as not to aggravate (or cause) a spinal injury. Doing so with this scrawny black cat was not easy, his long, spindly legs flopping everywhere.

I gingerly set him in the passenger seat.

Now what?

The year was 1994, before cell phones took over humanity.

It was early morning, sunrise time. My plan was to call my regular vet. But they were several miles away. If they were closed, I would have wasted time driving there and still have to find a vet. It would be better to find a phone, call around and confirm someplace was open before wasting time driving there.

I cruised around, searching for a payphone, hoping the cat wouldn't just die in my car.

Time was important. I didn't know how long the little guy would last.

The first payphone I found was about to be used by a woman. I explained the situation to her, my voice shaking.

"I have an injured at in my car," I said.

"This is an emergency call," she said and turned her back to me.

I suspected she was lying and just didn't want to give up the phone. I remember she had the coldest blue eyes. I considered shoving her aside, but I knew that would not help my (and the cat's) problem.

Plus, that would probably be considered bad form.

I said some words that should never be repeated and drove across the street to another phone.

Then I realized I had no change.

The problems we used to have.

I decided to take my chances. I dialed the operator and explained the situation. She kindly patched me through to my veterinarian's office for free, reminding me that not all strangers are callous, lying blue-eyed jerks with rocks for hearts.

Thank you, operator lady, wherever you are.

My vet was not open yet, but there were some in the office and of course they would handle an emergency. They wanted me to assure them I would take care of any bills resulting from the care.

A thought flashed across my mind: "How much money are we talking about here?"

My heart's pounding easily overruled my mind's worry.

"Of course I'll pay."

On the drive there, the cat rested his head.

"Don't go to sleep on me," I told him, lifting his head up multiple times. I feared he might have a concussion, and having suffered two as a boy falling out of trees, I recalled instructions to avoid sleep immediately after or you might never wake.

I arrived at the vet, cat still alive. He was rushed into the back.

Outside, I took time to breathe.

I did my part, I thought, it's out of my hands now.

The wait wasn't long. The vet called me in and showed me the x-ray.

I must confess that when doctors hit me with a lot of information, I lose focus and listen for keywords.

Give me the big picture, doc. Are the odds good or bad?

The cat had a chance. Or his lungs might fill with fluid, smothering his heart, and then he probably wouldn't survive.

In my simplifying mind, I figured he was giving the little guy a 50/50 chance.

Not good. Not bad.

I'd take those odds.

Signs Up Signs Down

I put out flyers and stuffed them in mailboxes on the street where I encountered the cat.

"Skinny black cat found. White dot on chest. Wearing a pink collar. Call if he's yours."

Then I waited. I checked in with the vet regularly and visited the cat.

I had already grown attached to him, and named him Arlo.

Days passed. Still no calls from the cat's owner. Good.

The only call was from the vet. Arlo was going to

make it. They filed down one of his fangs. It was broken in half in the accident, but they made it sharp and useful. His lower jaw was wired into one piece, and a couple metal rods were attached to his hip to repair his leg.

Several days passed without any calls from someone searching for a missing cat.

I made a special trip out at night and tore down all the signs.

Whatever his past was, whoever put the pink collar on him, will forever remain a mystery.

The vet hit me with a bill, and at the bottom they noted, 50% off for a "Good Samaritan" discount.

How nice!

The cost was still in the thousands. It was a lot for a young couple just starting out, but manageable.

That's why there's loan sharks. I mean credit cards. Borrow the money now, promise to pay it back later with a lot extra.

Some people are horrified at us animal-lovers when they learn how much we spend on our critter friends. I'm horrified right back at them.

As much as money is a constant pressure, when someone is your friend, you don't think about the cost.

If you're really in love, money means nothing.

Trouble at Home

Arlo survived. For the rest of his life, he had a strange walk, his injured right leg swinging out to the side in an arc. It was his signature strut but didn't slow him down.

I was excited. I had never saved a life before. I'd always loved those scenes in movies where the hero rushes into a burning building, explosions everywhere, rock soundtrack blaring, etc. and saves the day.

It wasn't like that, but it felt cool all the same. I felt

hero-ish.

We were excited to welcome a second cat to our family.

I finally got him home and Heather saw him for the first time.

"His eyes look too close together," she commented. In all the excitement, I hadn't got a good look at him. She was right. He was rail-thin, and his eyes seemed, well, too close together. He was so doped up on medicine he let out a singular howl that would have made a drunk coyote jealous.

Tovy (our other cat) and he were not getting along, spitting and swatting whenever they saw each other. This was not good with Arlo's many stitches.

They had to be separated. Somehow, we came to the agreement that I would sleep on the couch to keep Tovy company, and Heather slept in the sealed off bedroom with Arlo.

She tells the heartwarming tale of how in the middle of the night he got up from his improvised bed and with obvious extreme effort, through his pain and injuries, staggered onto the mattress and curled against her for warmth.

She became weepy, moved by his effort just to be at her side. It was enough to soften anyone's heart.

But then he peed.

All over the bed.

Which is enough to send anyone into a blind rage.

But we knew he'd been through a lot, so we kept a smile and washed everything.

* * *

Days later, we were watching television. Arlo was curled up on my lap. Things were getting normal.

I had to get up and gently pushed Arlo off me. I stood up.

"Did you wet your pants?" my wife asked, pointing to a stain in my lap.

As an adult, I don't often wet my pants, but I've been through enough to never say never.

But not this time. The stain in my lap had to have come from Arlo.

I grabbed him and that's when I saw the metal pipe poking out from his hip. The tubes holding his leg bones together while they healed had pierced through his skin.

It was gross but not as gory as it sounds.

We called the vet immediately.

He wasn't bleeding, but the pin poked out, offering a tiny window to the slick flesh just below his skin.

The vet advised it wasn't an emergency, just try to keep him immobile. Come in tomorrow to get it sewed up again.

Oh sure, keeping him immobile would be easy enough, I thought, I'll just put him in a cat carrier.

To anyone who has ever had the misfortune of attempting to store a cat in a carrier, you know this is a special kind of torment. Even with metal rods sticking out from under the skin, he fought and clawed and screamed. Once I finally won the battle, he hurled himself against the carrier's cage, howling with each charge.

I tried to comfort him by putting the carrier on my chest. If I couldn't let him lie on my lap, this was the best I could do. It looked as ridiculous as it sounds.

Arlo continued his thrashing, hurling his body against the cage, showing off his feral origins, pink collar or not. I tried to reach my fingers in to pet him, but he stuck his paw through the cage, claws out and pinned my finger against the bars, drawing blood.

I had visions of exposed his leg pin catching on the cage and ripping out of his skin. Yuck.

This was not working.

I let him out.

He wasn't bleeding, so it seemed he could survive the night.

I set a timer to wake every two hours to check on him.

I woke up, made sure he wasn't bleeding. Back to sleep for two hours. Woke up, no bleeding.

He lived through the night.

Somehow, so did I.

Responsibility After Saving A Life

There's a saying, a myth, a belief, an old legend?

One of those.

It goes like this: once you save someone's life you become responsible for them.

Shouldn't it be the other way around?

Why is the saver burdened with a lifetime of obligation? Shouldn't the saved owe the saver?

But maybe the saying isn't a command, maybe I recoil at this phrase because I naturally avoid anything that smells like work. And though I was glad to have saved Arlo, did that mean I had to constantly be on guard?

Regardless of the myth, that's how it worked out. Far more than any other cat I've lived with, I became obsessive about Arlo's health.

Other cats had their ups and downs and adventures, that I could handle as well as any cat parent, but none threw me into an emotional spiral like Arlo.

Kurt and his Shirt

We moved into a new apartment, bringing Arlo and Tovy with us.

In the home behind our building lived a friendly couple. We'll call the guy Kurt. He was one of those types who was very social.

Heather and I are those types who are very not.

Kurt got drunk a lot and talked to every passerby. He was a wonderful storyteller and we suspect he was illiterate, as Kurt and his wife, we'll call her Diane, were always arguing. She wanted to read, he wanted to drink and talk to people.

We were in that phase when you arrive at a new place, and people are wondering when would be a good time to say hello. Kurt was always out in the parking lot and we would wave, but we hadn't met him officially yet.

In the new place, Arlo would do this odd thing where he would roll upside down and stick his paw under the front door and rattle it.

He would then emit his bizarre meow-howl combination that we describe as "weeooo." It was the strangest meow we'd ever heard, and since I've never heard anything like it.

Usage example: "Arlo is weeooo-ing and rattling the door again!"

He seemed to want to go outside. Because I couldn't help but spoil him, I decided to try taking him on a walk. It was all very normal. A friendly couple avoiding the neighbors and taking their feral cat for a stroll on a leash.

On a leash?

Cat families out there are probably already chuckling. Cats plus leashes equal tears. And those tears do not come from the cat.

As we should have expected, Arlo flipped out and began pulling at the leash. Heather didn't want him to choke so she tried not to hold on too tight. This resulted in her spinning in a circle, Arlo thrashing around at the perimeter on his hind-legs like a monkey with fangs, his front paws grabbing the leash lead.

Olympic hammer throws. Think of that, but instead of a hunk of metal at the end, there's a snarling cat.

Heather spun and I chased.

Kurt, the new neighbor we'd been avoiding, saw us in the yard, spinning in circles, trying to wrangle but not strangle our skinny cat.

Arlo burst from the leash and took off.

Somehow, he got on top of a nearby two-story church.

We could see his little head poking over the edge, looking down on us. Taunting us. Just rubbing it in.

Neighbor Kurt saw his chance to associate with his socially-avoidant neighbors.

He came over and said, "I can climb up there and get your cat down."

That's how we finally officially met.

Oh no, we said. You don't have to do that. Please don't do that. If you fall you'll get hurt.

I ran inside and called the fire department. They said they wouldn't send a truck. They didn't do that for cats up a tree. Why? Are there some fires keeping you busy right now? You mean television lied to me?

Frustrated, I went back outside, to find Kurt had somehow gotten on the roof of the church and captured Arlo. He (meaning Kurt) took off his tank top, made a sling and put Arlo into it.

Shirtless, he held Arlo over the edge of the roof, bobbing him up and down.

What miracles had I missed while on the phone with

the fire company?

"See? I got him!" Kurt said. "I can lower him down!"

Yes, you can lower him, I thought, but there is no one below you to get him. There's still a good ten feet to the lower roof over the entrance.

A friendly chap from the fire company had heard about my call and strolled the few blocks over to see what was up. His official presence was enough to convince Kurt to come down.

Somehow Kurt did all this with Arlo, who again took off, but this time, right back into the apartment.

"Chaos achieved," he probably thought. "My work here is done. For now."

This is probably not the ideal way to meet the neighbors, but we ended up having many wonderful years with Kurt. I hope he's doing well wherever he is.

Last we heard, he and Diane had split up. It wasn't surprising, but still sad.

Ambassador Arlo Welcomes Some Strays

If you're thinking the incident with Kurt taught me the lesson that Arlo could not be controlled when taken outside, you'd be wrong.

If you think I'm a dumbass for not learning that lesson, you'd be right.

But I have a defense. It's not a good one, but hear me out. Innocent until proven guilty, unless of course it's the internet and then you're innocent or guilty based on whatever people feel.

As much as I love living with critters, I sometimes feel bad about domesticating them. As much as I can, I want them to be free.

I already explained how Arlo would do his thing where he would flop on his back and weeooo at the door. Then he would squeeze his little paw under the tiny space of the door and pull on it to make the door rattle.

It was incredibly and effectively annoying.

I'd "take him for a walk" and stroll alongside him in the lobby of our apartment building, sometimes even taking him outside. I didn't use a leash because that disaster led to Kurt on the church roof and Arlo wearing Kurt's shirt. If I don't use a leash then the leash can't cause trouble, right?

As I say it out loud, its appearance of logic but complete lack of sense is obvious.

This was a disaster waiting to happen.

Disaster didn't wait long.

We're strolling around outside, and suddenly, Arlo takes off like a bullet, his forever injured leg not slowing him at all.

He had spotted a kitten nearby and chased the little guy up a tree. Also snarled and growled at the white and gray baby. Owing to his small size, the kitten was able back way out on the end of a bending branch, while Arlo is closer in toward the trunk, making bizarre howling and other frightening aggression noises.

I couldn't get him down.

He just kept yowling. The kitten was way out on the end if this thin branch bending under his weight.

I'm afraid to throw something, lest the kitten fall. I'm calling Arlo and cursing at him, but no luck. The tree is too small for me to climb. This is a stupid mess, and I'm getting nowhere.

And it's getting dark. I'm going to have to leave Arlo outside in the dark.

It's all my fault.

I concede I am an idiot.

As I am prone to do during distress, I decide to take a nap.

I left Arlo outside, still snarling at the kitten on the end of branch in a stalemate.

Why did my guy have to get all territorial?

When I wake up, Heather has solved it all.

She went outside and patiently waited for Arlo to come down.

Then she went back out to see how the kitten was.

He and his mother showed up and the two of them ran around her in circles.

This is a delightful image to visualize.

I see the cats performing a pagan ritual, and the local nature-witch hippie watching them calmly.

She passed the test.

Somewhere in our apartment were two new cats to adopt.

Arlo and the mother cat (we named her April) became good friends, adorably sleeping snuggled together for the rest of their lives.

The kitten we named Zappa after musician Frank Zappa.

Our cat family had doubled in one night.

Thanks a lot, Arlo.

Arlo On Fire

Once, while I was writing, Arlo was attacking the junk I had on my desk. At this time, he was swatting at a rubber band and a paper clip. Being the persistent pain the ass he was, he would not stop.

I gently brushed him backwards, completely forgetting that I had a lit candle on my desk. I accidentally pushed him backwards right into it and his tail, just above his butthole, caught fire.

I gasped in horror, and as sudden loud sounds do to cats, this terrified him.

In a panic he jumped off the desk and took off, tail

and behind on fire.

He was easy to track as he left a smoke trail through the apartment.

Fortunately, the speed at which he ran had snuffed the flames.

I caught up to him and patted down his tail. Arlo-fur ashes went all over the floor.

It all happened in just a few seconds. Just a few moments of terror.

But the memories last a lifetime.

Arlo Saves the Day

I can't remember the specifics, but I was extremely sad.

I was sitting on the edge of the bathtub, staring at my feet, soaking in a fog of depression. I doubt there was a reason why. It's just how I felt.

Arlo appeared and kept rubbing against my legs, purring like crazy, occasionally looking up at me expectantly, helpfully.

His purring was loud. Very loud.

After a while, all I could hear was the purring.

How was I supposed to stay miserable with him making so much noise?

It was as if my sorrow was a brick wall. The vibrations of his incessant purring broke the stone into pebbles and the pebbles into dust. He destroyed that brick in a way a mighty blow never could.

I felt strange, and wonderful, as if through the gentlest surgery, my pain was removed.

Livin' in a Lead Box

Arlo's skill at racking up medical bills ran throughout his life.

His damaged canine fang from the accident that brought us together eventually had to be removed. For several hundred dollars, as it was infected.

He developed hyperthyroid, undergoing an expensive radiation treatment where he had to be kept in a lead box for a week and his poop was radioactive. I drove him to the University of Pennsylvania veterinary hospital and had him checked in.

A week later they cleared him.

He came home and it seemed nothing at all had changed.

Dreams of Heaven

I sometimes wonder about heaven.

In my version of heaven, every dog and cat I've loved is there.

My body has given up and I emerge beyond the field of reeds, and there they are, bounding toward me, bright, shining, as eager to see me as I am to see them.

A stampede of long-domesticated lions and wolves are rushing toward me. Overhead is a single crow. That's another story.

Of course, Arlo is there, among the crowd, his damaged right leg swinging out to the side as usual.

I sometimes wonder, do animals dream of heaven?

Do they dream of heaven in the same way we humans do?

Did Arlo think of sunbeams all day, his girl April curled up next to him?

And if so, am I there?

Does he dream that I will emerge and come to him?

I truly hope so.

Disappearing

Well into his senior years, Arlo vanished.

He was gone.

He wasn't in his usual spots. He wasn't outside. I ran

around in a panic.

I had saved him and I was responsible for him, and now, years and years since his accident, I had lost him.

I ran up and down the street, asking those passing by if they'd seen a black cat with a white dot on the chest, with three fangs and strange walk.

No. No. And Nope.

I ran around, frantic for an hour or two, hurling furniture aside, looking for some new hiding spot. I tried everything until I realized there was nothing, absolutely nothing more I could do.

I didn't want him to be gone.

I didn't save his life so many years ago from being hit by a car for him to go outside a decade later and get hit by a car. How could I let this happen?

I had searched everywhere.

I collapsed on the bed, helpless.

And then, suddenly, he comes strolling out of the closet.

Just like that.

As if to say, "Oh, hello." As casually as... I don't know, as casually as a purring cat.

I had looked in that closet a dozen times before running all over the world to find him, but he used his evil cat skill to hide.

He had to have heard me calling him.

He had to have heard the chaos of me tearing apart the place looking for him.

Why not just come out?

Let me know you're okay, then go back into the closet and have another twenty-hour nap?

Why let me suffer like that?

Of course, he had no answer.

It was as if nothing had happened. I flopped backwards on the bed and laughed hysterically.

The Last Day

One day, well into his later years, without much warning, Arlo stopped eating. He stopped drinking.

He sat in the basement, not moving.

I had seen this before in too many cats. He was dying. Rather than wait for his body to break down to a point where he was genuinely and obviously suffering, I called the vet.

We all knew. Arlo's time had come.

I remember that last hour, sitting on the loveseat in the basement with Arlo beside me, while I read a book. I wasn't going to make a fuss. I wasn't going to beg any god for a few more minutes. To do so would have been greedy and seemed ungrateful.

We had so many years we weren't supposed to have… and now I wanted more? How much more?

Forever was impossible and that would have been the only acceptable answer.

With all my might I tried to convince myself that this much had been enough.

I almost got myself to believe it.

For as much drama and noise and chaos as he caused, I expected more of the same for his exit, but no. Arlo just sat there, doing nothing but breathing. I sat next to him.

He howled once in the car on the way to the vet. I realized it was the first time I had heard him vocalize in a week. It was the last thing he ever said. It sounded like something was hurting him. Or maybe he was sad, or maybe he hated the car ride.

Probably all of those. There was no way to know.

The only thing I was sure of was that his time was up.

After

For a long time, I didn't think of him.

There was a great silence and a sad calm quiet in the air and in my mind.

Arlo's body had given out at last. The daily sounds and lunacy were replaced by a boring silence.

I knew I would remember him always, and I wanted to memorialize him in some way.

Eventually, I settled on the idea of a tattoo on my leg on the calf, where cats around the world often greet human friends by rubbing against them. He would be the ambassador to cats greeting me, for the rest of my life.

I couldn't find the art that felt right.

I didn't search too hard. It was all too painful.

Then maybe a year, two, I'm not sure. I stumbled on it. Just what I had been looking for. A piece of clip art on the internet that looked a lot like a symbol of Arlo might look. A little like an Egyptian hieroglyph. The cat was solid black, and the tattoo artist added a white dot on his chest easy enough.

The image was perfect.

He's in my heart, in the same way as every friend who has gone before him is. In the same way I hope to be when my time comes.

After the tattoo, I felt that strange emotion we refer to as "closure."

It's that feeling when something all feels done and in its right place, or at least a place that no longer itches, burns, or aches. A place that doesn't require any more adjustment. Where everything is done. The story of Arlo was complete.

I had paid him and the cat-kingdom the proper respect.

Now every cat I ever live with, and will ever live

with, will know how much they mean to me via a symbol etched into the skin of my calf.

Ambassador Arlo was the one I wanted to carry with me.

Let the symbol on my leg serve as a sign to the feline species.

Should I ever be traveling in a distant land and stray cat sees that tattoo, they'll know it's safe, even wise to go rub against this human's leg.

He seems all right…

…for a human.

The Cat, the Myth, the Legend

I've lived with a fair amount of non-humans at this point in my life. I've been there for most of their lives. From close to their birth to their death. I've had a lot of time to think about what it all means. I've had lots of practice in losing a loved one.

Here's what I'm thinking.

There is a phase after life.

Not as many believe, as a post-death life as literal as our current life. I think of it as a very real, but a more subtle second act.

When someone transitions from physical to something else: a legend.

A myth. A memory. A story that we remember. A presence we never forget.

After life, we become stories. Or more strongly, legends.

It's a transition that makes sense.

The body is gone but the legend lives on.

I like to think of anyone's passing that way. It makes it less painful. It seems complete.

Arlo's body wore out, but his memory lives on, his actions live on, the impact he had on me lives on.

So rather than say "He died," I prefer to say, "He became legend."

That he did.

47

ONE NIGHT IN SEXYLAND

WARNING: The following involves discussions of sex.

I know that may upset some folks. I'm not sure why.

People are overjoyed at the birth of a child, or at a marriage. All that means is that — unless you're in some weird cult — sex has already happened and/or more sex is on the way!

Look around. There are people everywhere, zillions of people all over the place, getting in your way, making traffic, making noise. Some say there are too many people.

You know what that means?

Lots and lots and lots of sex is happening.

I'm sorry if you picked up this collection of essays expecting some sort of family-friendly dribble because of my offbeat story about a quirky feline friend. Now suddenly you're horrified that we're going to talk about sex.

Let me gently remind you: that cat existed because his cat parents had sex. I'm here because my parents had sex, you're here because your parents had sex. We're all here because someone had sex, except maybe the for the A.I. that is reading this to feed its large language model database.

Everyone welcome Studbot 6000.

The point I've dry-humped for several paragraphs now is that we're all here because people had sex.

Despite the overlap between incels and Nazis, it is likely that even Hitler had sex.

Some people just don't like to talk about sex because it's (usually) a private activity. If that's you, please skip this chapter and continue to lie to yourself that everyone arrived via mail in a perfect bundle packaged lovingly by the wee baby savior or online retailer of your choice.

I don't mean to sound condescending. What I'm saying is if sex isn't your bag, skip this entry.

Oh, and if you don't like drugs, you should probably bail out too.

For the rest of you, onward.

Amsterdam

Amsterdam 2005. Ah yes! Long before marijuana became sort-of-legal in the USA, Amsterdam was the place you could go to smoke in peace, without fear of a decades long jail sentence.

You could do many other things legally, too, such as visit prostitutes.

Amsterdam seemed to me a kind of Las Vegas of Europe with much less lighting.

Also, Anne Frank's house was there.

Now I don't know if Vegas has something comparable to the tiny attic where the Frank girls hid from Nazis. But the way the USA is going at this time, it could be any day now.

For now, both are cities for commoners to pursue adults-only entertainment.

I was surprised to find that in addition to marijuana their headshops sold hallucinogenic mushrooms!

Was there no end to this city's delights?

I was pleased because I'm always looking to add to my drug-ingesting resume but at the same time I don't want to cause any permanent damage. As child of the 80s who endured the harshest propaganda of the USA's War on Drugs, I'm not as adventurous as I'd like to be. I was delighted that a little safety how-to pamphlet came with every magic mushroom packet. You could purchase your drugs in a store as simply as purchasing a pack of gum in the USA.

I had only been to Europe once in my life right out of high school. To show how old I am, this was before the European Union was a thing, and we needed to get visas for every damn country. Somewhere in my attic I still have a box with the coins of the different currencies from the several countries we visited.

Here we were in 2005, over a decade later. I wanted to go with my wife, Heather who had never been to Europe. I wanted to show her the world!

Sort of.

We teamed up with a friend who happened to be gay. We'll call him Jerry.

Amsterdam is a gay-friendly place he was eager to visit.

The three of us set out on a daring adventure.

The Red Light District

For those who don't know, Amsterdam is famous for its red light district. That part of town that features legal, or at least what is described as "decriminalized" prostitution.

Walk the cramped cobblestone streets, and the canals that prevent the city from drowning, and you can expect to pass by the normal stores, bars, cafes.

But once you hit the red light district, you'll know it.

You'll see glass doors built into the sides of the buildings. Behind the glass doors are small chambers, the back halves hidden by curtains, and lit by red lights, filling the tiny room with pink. In these workspaces are women, dressed only in their underwear, ready to have sex for money.

Being faithfully and happily married, this wasn't my gig, but it was fascinating to see.

Heather insists that when I saw my first red light woman I shrieked and turned away.

This is probably true.

I rounded a corner, and owing to the full height glass doors, I was suddenly within arms-reach of a woman wearing nothing but her underwear.

What else could a good Catholic boy from New Jersey do but cry out in fear?

These thin alleyways offered window-shopping of the strangest sort. Often several in a row, all with different shapes, sizes, colors of women. If you're wondering, at the time, I saw no men prostitutes. At least, no obviously male ones.

Our favorite avenue to walk offered five red-light doors across the street from a centuries-old church. It was a study in contrasts. Or a convenience for both groups.

The weekend crowds packed the streets, making progress through the darker red-light zones a shoulder-to-shoulder affair.

Suited businessmen from the far east traveled in quiet packs, murmuring to each other. Loud British lads called out "Oi! Oi! Hampshire boys!" or whatever to find each other. And there was every other kind of person in between. Folks from all over the world had come to see, and perhaps partake of, Amsterdam's red-light district.

Besides the dense crowds, I remember passing a doorway where the woman was chewing a handful of M&Ms with an open mouth. She had a pile of the candies in her palm. She saw me looking, perhaps a bit too long, and laughed, holding out her hand to offer some.

How nice.

The Night of Nights
Jerry was eager to go to a club.

Heather wanted to get another tattoo to add to her already-extensive ink.

Me? This was before decent GPS tech and I was apparently the only one willing and/or capable of reading a map, so my task was to make sure everyone got do what they wanted.

We searched for a tattoo shop.

The first place we explored was a stereotype of all things European. The artist was hunched over, dressed all in black, a hood covering most of her head. When she saw us waiting, she barked, "Don't touch anything," her thick accent bubbling with contempt. I suspected the tattoo in this gloomy place came with a free infection.

We continued our quest and found a shop that was well-lit, clean, with friendly artists.

Like the best of Europeans, these artists were friendly and spoke an impressive array of languages. Whatever tourist came in, they were greeted in their language. French, English, Dutch, German, and I don't know what else. It was hard not to like these guys. They were so friendly and so… multi-lingual. I was jealous of the ease with which they switched languages.

We Americans are big on individuality as isolation, but that's not how one becomes stronger. When we withdraw from the world, we get dumber, and we're already doing great there. The USA's dumbass demographic keeps crying for us to be English mono-linguals, but the more we do that, the more we're left out and left behind.

Heather sat in the tattoo recliner as muscular, tattooed, charming, poly-lingual Euro-dudes tended to her. Pleased that she would be safe, I was ready to guide Jerry to his club.

We found the place with surprising ease and Jerry gave the all clear. I told him to have fun and raced back to Heather before some Eurobro stole her.

We were still on USA time, so being a night owl was easy. Our bodies were just entering the evening, but the time in the Amsterdam was almost midnight.

This day being a weekday, I was alone in the dark and recently rained-upon rocky streets.

I slowed down, an idea forming.

Wait a sec.

Jerry is at the club. Heather's getting a tattoo.

If tonight was the night of solo adventures. I needed to do something.

But what?

If my life was a movie, that would have been the moment the glowing neon sign of "Sexyland" emerged from the fog. It would radiate in the mist accompanied by the sound of a church choir singing a glorious wordless tone.

Ahhhhh!

Sexyland!

I had no idea what this place was, but the name was

irresistible. There was no multiverse timeline where any version of myself was going to pass by a place labeled "Sexyland" and not investigate.

When Jerry got back to our rented bedbug apartment from his club he would have stories, when Heather got her tattoo and was finished, she would have stories.

They would then turn to me and ask, "What did you do?"

I would have a one-word answer.

Sexyland.

I didn't know what it was. My thought process was shaky, owing to the endless amounts of marijuana, mushrooms, and coffee we were consuming.

Nervous as could be, unsure what I would find, I entered.

So Many Options at Sexyland

Sexyland was dark inside. And there was no concierge to guide me.

My footsteps made that ripping sound when you walk along a rubber floor that is perpetually sticky. I was immediately grossed out, but such is the price for adventure. I continued.

A quick note. Obviously, I intended to and would be faithful to my wife. Whatever carnal delights Sexyland held, I would not violate the trust and terms of our relationship. I say this only as a matter of public record, not as a judgmental humblebrag, but I guess it works as both.

I get that every relationship is different. If a couple wants to be free with intimate relations and still be companions, that's their business. If everyone consents and is aware and honest and happy, good for them.

While I didn't know what Sexyland had in store, physical intimacy with another was out of bounds.

Gross, unappealing public sights for the sake of experience were okay.

Visual observation is acceptable, something Heather reminds of every time Jason Momoa graced our TV screen.

"Hey hey hey."

My point is, I didn't go into Sexyland with the intent to have sex with anyone. I went in with the intent to explore. I would never break a commitment to my best friend.

That's not to imply that opportunities are being thrown at me. Women aren't beckoning me to have sex with them. That would be ridiculous.

(That's foreshadowing, btw. You'll see.)

Okay, fine. Shut up. Get to the good stuff.

Get back to Sexyland.

The place was completely dark, a windowless box and no lights but the glow of video screens. Like any modern human, I obediently walked toward them, drawn by the light.

The screens were set in wooden cases like old school arcade cabinets. Small barriers were between each cabinet for minimal privacy. On the console there was a joystick (resist pun) and a bunch of buttons. The screen was divided into four sections. Choose your own porn adventure. There was a little dispenser for napkins.

Gross, yuck, eww, and… OMG in a bad way.

Previews of four different porn films showed in each quadrant of the screen. None were appealing. In fact, they were downright repulsive. It was all way too hardcore for me.

So far, this was a swing and a miss.

What else you got for me, Sexyland?

The Live Sex show

A what now?

A LIVE SEX SHOW? Happening soon? What luck!

I don't know a single person who has ever attended a live sex show. I did see the play O, Calcutta! a long time ago but I'm not sure that counts. They were naked, if I recall. No live sex.

Again, I entered a tiny private booth. This one ended with an opaque window. I put in a Euro coin and the window became transparent. The nerdy part of my brain flared and wondered how they did that. Here I am in Sexyland and I'm focused on the tech.

Anyway, I could now see into a small round chamber. Other viewing windows surrounded the perimeter.

Fortunately, I was the only one in attendance.

Just like that, the live sex show began! A man and woman entered the chamber wearing only underwear and the floor started rotating!

Whoa! That took me by surprise. It may not sound like much, but you probably (and unfortunately?) do not have a head full of pot, mushrooms, and coffee. In that state, I was overly impressed with the rotating floor. So much so that I thought about it as the show began.

Anyway, the guy and gal pawed at each other pulled on their minimal clothes.

It was the foreplay to love-making in a movie that wants to keep its rating PG-13. At this point the star of the show remained the room-sized Lazy Susan.

She was the only one working the whole time. The other two were phoning it in.

After a minute or two of basic cable pre-sex, the window fogged over.

I quickly fumbled in my pocket for another Euro coin.

Once I could see through the window once again, the man and woman are touching and licking – simulated, I might add.

I was close enough that without the wall and glass I could have reached out and touched them. Not that I would want to. But they were that close, spinning around for a full panoramic view.

I wondered if they ever got dizzy.

My brain seemed to focus on these details other than the sex that was not happening. Auto-transparent windows? Interesting. Rotating floor? How cool.

Oh yes, and two people about to have sex right in front of me? Meh.

But there was only more touching and simulating and… nothing.

Window fogs, coin goes in.

How about that floor!

Still just some long-distance pawing and licking.

Most of you out there probably recognize by now this is a hustle. Somewhere in my foggy thoughts, I knew it too, but I had limited Euro coins and even more limited brain capacity at the time. I played along. How far would they go? I could only be burned for so much before my pocket was empty.

Let's see what they get up to.

Window dark. Another coin. More barely touching. Another coin.

I started to feel like a genuine pervert, because I'm thinking to myself, get to the good stuff, damn it! I don't have all night! I'm not made of Euros! Some dude could be charming my wife as we speak! You gotta give me something!

In goes the last coin and…more of the same fake touching.

The windows turns solid and I bang my fist on the

frame.

"Damn it!"

I was frustrated, not furious.

Then I felt extremely pathetic, like I was a sex junkie denied my fix.

I stood there before the opaque window chuckling at myself like any good weirdo.

For all I know those two folks are still in there. Still spinning, still taking their time getting to first base.

The positive I take from the experience is proving I'm not a natural at the pervier side of life. The grossness was such a turnoff I couldn't get genuinely aroused.

Not that you needed to know that.

Before Sexyland, I had been to a strip club once in my life. Twenty-years on and that stat still holds.

I hated the strip club. It was icky. There were only two women in the place and tons of guys. Obviously, it was safe to assume all the dudes were rocking hard-ons. Owing to the lopsided girl-guy ratio, the experience seemed sprinkled with a fairy dust of homoeroticism.

Nothing wrong with homosexuality of course, but that whole scene just isn't for me.

Sexyland was an obligation.

How could I not go to a place with a name like that?

Ah, the power of marketing.

Just one more thing to do.

But oh, the memories!

See, when I travel, I like to collect random objects to remember fun times. Not plastic crap in a gift shop, but genuine reminders. Nothing fancy, just ticket stubs, receipts, stickers, coasters, etc. Little tokens and accidental souvenirs to serve as trophies from an adventure.

I went outside and around to Sexyland's front booth, where this enormous guy was behind glass, counting the cash for the night. He looked like a bouncer, and his Dutch-ness made him more intimidating.

You know what I mean, my fellow Americans. The way Europeans talk, if that accent is anywhere east of France and north of Italy, it sounds angry.

Dutch, German, Polish, Russian, etc. It all sounds harsh and grumpy.

I knew I was testing my luck when I knocked on the window and spoke to the enormous fellow.

"Do you have a business card?"

I needed a doodad. A knickknack. A thingy. And business cards were the easiest and cheapest way to get one. Sexyland didn't seem to have receipts (smart!) and there was no merch store (dumb!).

Who wouldn't want a sticker "Sexyland" on their scooter helmet, beanie copter, or laptop computer? But without those, I'd settle for a business card. They are free and most profitable enterprises have them.

I asked again. "Do you have a business card?"

This enormous Dutch dude, who looks like he could have been or was, an MMA fighter, or at least a club bouncer, ignores me. He keeps counting the cash, head down, bent over the till, flipping bills with his thumb.

Oh no, sir. You do not ignore an American. No, you do not.

I knocked on the plexiglass again.

"Excuse me. Do you have a business card?"

I am convinced now he is purposefully ignoring me. I found that rude. It was only after I sobered up weeks later, back in the States, that I realized I might have been the rude one. Hans was just trying to keep the cash count in his head.

Some things are obvious when you're not stoned for

days on end.

At the time, I was not having it.

Knock knock.

"Do you have a business card?"

And he finally answered, turning his head just slightly.

"No."

But it wasn't just a "No."

It was Dutch no. In a Dutch accent. With an international tone. It was a NO on many different levels, as in, "No, you dumbass, we don't have a business card for Sexyland. No, I will not be talking to you anymore. No, I will not hesitate to pound you into the piss-soaked cobblestones you're standing on if you insist on interrupting me while I'm counting the money. Knock on the window one more time and find out."

There was a whole lot of No in that one No.

I got the message.

I walked away, thinking. Huh. That's odd. Every business should have a business card.

Had Hans been friendlier I could have provided him some feedback on his customer service.

Oh well. I'd have to rely on my memory to commemorate my night in Sexyland.

Once I got over Hans' lack of business acumen, I immediately panicked. How much time had passed?

Owing to a head full of additional chemicals, I had no idea.

I've got to rescue my wife from charming Euro-dudes!

Damsel(s) in Distress

I'm wandering the dark, recently rained-on walkways of central Amsterdam. The streets have names at least 20 letters long. For my monolingual American brain, currently floating in a vat of magic mushroom and THC stew, that's way too much to remember.

Even if I try to just recall the first few letters, I get confused. Then again, I didn't exactly remember where the tattoo shop was. So even understanding the street names wouldn't have helped.

I'm wandering and hoping.

It's dark and late on a mid-weekday, so it's a slow night for the red-light ladies. Alone, with no one else around, I pass a row of doors, all five of the women step out and beckon to me. The opening of the doors at roughly the same time vaguely reminiscent of a Broadway musical.

"Come here, come on! Come on," they call out.

I get nervous and tongue-tied around pretty ladies, but I also believe in being polite, so I stammer as I respectfully decline. And I feel like it's good manners to explain.

"Uh, I'm married. I do appreciate the offer. Uh, thank you. Uh, no."

I speedwalk past them all.

"But it will be fuuuun!"

I like to think that the silent 500-year-old church nearby was surprised that I didn't give in to such a riot of temptation. If one of its gargoyles could talk, it would say to the other, if that other one could hear. "Stuck here for centuries. First time I've seen that."

"He's either really faithful, or really gay."

"Good point."

I found my way back to the tattoo place.

Somehow.

And all was well at least for one night.

One of My Favorite Panic Attacks

One night while Jerry was off on his own, Heather and

I went to a coffee shop for a delightful date.

I went to the barista, bud-tender, bartender hostess and said, "I want a space cake."

She handed me a menu.

They had a menu!

At the time, this blew my mind. This was before I was aware there were hundreds of strains of marijuana that offer different types of highs. I didn't know what all the options meant, so I handed the menu back and casually said, "Give me the strongest thing you've got."

And then we ate a space cake. A chocolate cake infused with hash, which if I understand it, is basically marijuana concentrated to make it more powerful.

We smoked a joint and drank coffee.

This was going to be great!

But it wasn't.

We went to another coffeeshop, decorated in a beautiful dark wood interior. It was an ideal little café to relax and let the chemicals do the driving.

But I felt my heart racing.

The electro music was thumping and suddenly I couldn't take it.

I don't know what I mean by that. I just couldn't.

If "I can't even," was a phrase back then, that's what I would have felt. Just an inarticulate uncomfortableness with existing. The unbearable beingness of being.

I was upset, scared, and nervous, without any reason to be.

"We have to leave," I said to Heather.

"What?"

"We have to leave NOW!"

I took a step off the barstool. My foot hit the floor in complete darkness.

* * *

I was out in the streets again. Heather was at my side.

How I got there was a complete mystery to me. How much time had passed, I had no idea.

Whatever happened in those moments, I would have to rely on Heather to tell me.

"You freaked out, knocked over your stool and ran from the place," she said. "I found you outside."

"How long has it been?"

"Just a couple minutes."

"Oh."

I was embarrassed about making a tiny scene as a dumb tourist, but a tipped over stool wasn't too bad.

What was bad was that I was having a panic attack.

My heart was thundering as we wandered the streets.

I thought I might die.

We got back to the apartment.

These days, I know what a panic attack is, and I can fend it off with intentional breathing.

But then, I spent my time lying on the bed-bug infested mattress of our rental flat thinking I was going to die.

Jerry and Heather insisted I wouldn't and kept laughing about it in my face. After a few hours I came back down.

What a fun vacation!

Zay-ein! Zay-ein!

Our Amsterdam adventure was during the early days of the internet. Pornographic call-in lines were still popular, before they were replaced by online videos and chat rooms and all the tech the web has to offer.

Late at night you would see TV ads talking about phone numbers you could call for sex talk.

The scripts were all very similar. Something like this.

"Call and talk to sexy girls. Our hot and ready babes are just — unnnh! — waiting to hear you come … to the phone. Call one-whatever-six nine six nine."

These ads were everywhere and they littered the back of newspapers.

Now I hear you young ones out there asking, "Like, uh, what's a newspaper?" Think of it as an app on paper that changed only once a day. Barbaric, I know. But it was all we had.

Anyway, it turns out Jerry is one of those people who puts the TV on at night and lets it run while he's in bed. The white noise of it all helps him sleep.

Good for him, not so good for me.

Late night Dutch TV was no different that late night American TV. They had the same type of ads for sex-phone-lines, only these were in Dutch.

I awake in the middle of the night to the sound of some Dutch woman gasping as if she's having the most amazing intimate encounter in all of history. She goes on about hot and ready babes just waiting for me to come… to the phone.

In Dutch.

I can't understand the words, but I understand the breathless tone and the images just fine.

The phone number at the end of these ads was always something easy to remember or some combination of 69 – which for the puritans out there who don't know – is a sex position.

I'm unable to sleep. Because all I can hear is this, nonstop: "Blah blah blahstraatenweegen blah blah blah" but when they get to the number, as on American TV, our narrator lady goes all in.

ZAY EIN ZAY EIN

I figure it's One-whatever-6969 or 0202 or whatever in Dutch. Or something like that. And to this day, as I write this, I can STILL hear it. Just the last part of the number where the woman really puts all her acting talents. And like the American ads they repeat the number at least 17 times during the 30 second ad. Which is then followed by a nearly identical 30 second ad.

Blah-blah-blahblahblah-ZAY-EIN-ZAY-EIN. Blah-blah-unhhh!-blah-blah! ZAY-EIN ZAY-EIN.

I can't sleep.

Over and over and over. ZAY-EIN ZAY-EIN.

I will probably never unhear it. In the future when I'm on my deathbed and they are going to upload my consciousness into the great computer, my dying synapses will fire at random.

And among the memories forever burned into that code is the sound of a buxom blonde woman, twisting a telephone cord around her finger as she parts her cherry red lips, gasping.

ZAY EIN ZAY EIN.

Forever and ever.

ZAY EIN ZAY EIN.

48

SEARCHING FOR HUMOR

As I was nearing the end of writing this book, I ventured into a bookstore, looking to size up the competition.

As usual, I had begun this project in the worst possible way, following my creative passion instead of planning and researching the landscape first. That's what smart writers call "writing to market." They see what's out there, what's selling, and they let that determine what they write.

I follow my heart and advocate for this swashbuckling attitude via the following spin: "I don't like to be controlled by trends or capitalism."

That sounds great! Very bold and artsy! But I have to remind myself, if I don't consider the market at first, I'm not allowed to cry if sales results aren't what I want.

Of course, all this explanation implies some degree of thought went into this venture. Instead, I implemented my usual course of action, a tactic I like to call "leap before you look." It's good for the heart, bad for the mind.

"I've got an idea," I thought one day, "Sure, I've written thrillers and horror shorts before, but this time I'll write a humor book about my silly adventures and loopy viewpoints!" Now, nearly done, it was well past time to assess what authors I'd be up against.

In the massive bookstore, I couldn't find the humor books. I had to ask for help.

Oh, there it was, a small, single section of shelves stuffed in a quiet corner, all alone.

It felt like a sign of the times. No one was focused on free-range happiness, weird wild joy. The books that took up the store were instead concerned with fighting via politics and ideology. The other big genre was happiness made out to be work, a job with a list of tasks to do, journals to fill, checklists and special pens. All manner of ways to find joy so long as you bought the right gadgets and installed the correct apps.

Was I being foolish to write a book of creative nonfiction silliness with such a small market?

Or was it wise to do so? Was I accidentally applying what business dorks call a "blue ocean strategy"? Meaning, to enter a field with minimal competition? Do what few others are so you more easily stand out?

In these terrible depressing times (which seem to be all times) were people so obsessed with survival and combat (both cultural and literal) that they didn't take time to laugh?

Maybe.

We'll find out.

Or maybe we just did.

And for that, dearest reader, I thank you.

49

THANKS ALL AROUND

If you've read this far, I want to say thank you again. If you've skipped ahead to this page, aw heck, thank you, too, ya cheater. I would ask anyone reading this to please leave a review of this book on your favorite website retailer.

Tell your friends. Tell your enemies. Independent writers need your recommendations since we lack the budget to take out full-page ads in snooty New York City magazines and peer-pressure a whole society into reading the latest literary sensation, and lying about how they understood and/or loved it.

If you help spread the word about this book, I would consider you to be an even more superb person! That's tough to do because I already think highly of you!

If want to reach the greatest heights of awesomeness (in my view, anyway) visit my website LarryNocella.com, where you'll get a free eBook for joining the mailing list. Then any time I post something it will come right to your email! It's free and you can subscribe at any time.

I keep this record of sexy, smart folks like yourself just to stay in touch. I don't sell your email or your data. I would never do such a thing. Thank you again and I hope to hear from you soon, my fellow oddball!

Larry Nocella

www.ingramcontent.com/pod-product-compliance
Lightning Source LLC
Chambersburg PA
CBHW060317050426
42449CB00011B/2517